LifeLight

"In Him was life, and the life was the light of men." John 1:4

Obadiah/Jonah/Micah

LEADERS GUIDE

CONCORDIA PUBLISHING HOUSE • SAINT LOUIS

The prophet Micah looks on as the Holy Spirit, in bodily form as a dove, descends upon the Virgin Mary. "From you," the Lord declares through the prophet, "shall come forth for Me one who is to be ruler in Israel" (Micah 5:2). The Flemish master Hubert van Eyck has added Mary's reply to the angel upside down as though it were written for the heavenly host. "Behold, I am the servant of the Lord" (Luke 1:38), she says, with world-changing humility. So we see what a major contribution these so-called Minor Prophets make to the unfolding wonders of God's salvation. *(The Prophet Micah and the Virgin Annunciate, detail from the exterior of the left wing of the Ghent Altarpiece, St. Bavo Cathedral, Ghent, Belgium.)*

3558 S. Jefferson Ave., St. Louis, MO 63118-3968
1-800-325-3040 • www.cph.org

Written by Roland Cap Ehlke

Edited by Edward A. Engelbrecht

Cover: The Ghent Altarpiece (1425–32), Hubert van Eyck, detail. Iberfoto / Iberfoto

This publication may be available in Braille, in large print, or on cassette tape for the visually impaired. Please allow 8 to 12 weeks for delivery. Write to Lutheran Braille Workers, P.O. Box 5000, Yucaipa, CA 92399; call toll-free 1-800-925-6092; or visit the Web site: www.LBWinc.org.

Manufactured in the United States of America

1 2 3 4 5 6 7 8 9 10 24 23 22 21 20 19 18 17 16 15

Contents

Introduction

Welcome to LifeLight

A special pleasure is in store for you. You will be instrumental in leading your brothers and sisters in Christ closer to Him who is our life and light (John 1:4). You will have the pleasure of seeing fellow Christians discover new insights and rediscover old ones as they open the Scriptures and dig deep into them, perhaps deeper than they have ever dug before. More than that, you will have the pleasure of sharing in this wonderful study.

LifeLight—An In-depth Study

LifeLight is a series of in-depth Bible studies. The goal of LifeLight is that through a regular program of in-depth personal and group study of Scripture, more and more Christian adults may grow in their personal faith in Jesus Christ, enjoy fellowship with the members of His body, and reach out in love to others in witness and service.

In-depth means that this Bible study includes the following four components: individual daily home study; discussion in a small group; a lecture presentation on the Scripture portion under study; and an enhancement of the week's material (through reading the enrichment magazine).

LifeLight Participants

LifeLight participants are adults who desire a deeper study of the Scriptures than is available in the typical Sunday morning adult Bible class. (Mid-to-older teens might also be LifeLight participants.) While LifeLight does not assume an existing knowledge of the Bible or special experience or skills in Bible study, it does assume a level of commitment that will bring participants to each of the nine weekly assemblies having read the assigned readings and attempted to answer the study questions. Daily reading and study will require from 15 to 30 minutes for the five days preceding the LifeLight assembly. The day following the assembly will be spent reviewing the previous week's study by going over the completed study leaflet and the enrichment magazine.

LifeLight Leadership

While the in-depth process used by LifeLight begins with individual study and cannot achieve its aims without this individual effort, it cannot be completed by individual study alone. Therefore, trained leaders are necessary. You fill one or perhaps more of the important roles described below.

The Director

This person oversees the LifeLight program in a local center (which may be a congregation or a center operated by several neighboring congregations). The director

- serves as the parish LifeLight overall coordinator and leader;
- coordinates the scheduling of the LifeLight program;
- orders materials;
- convenes LifeLight leadership-team meetings;
- develops publicity materials;
- recruits participants;
- maintains records and budgeting;
- assigns, with the leadership-team, participants to small discussion groups;
- makes arrangements for facilities;
- communicates outreach opportunities to small-group leaders and to congregational boards;
- follows up on participants who leave the program.

The Assistant Director *(optional)*

This person may assist the director. Duties listed for the director may be assigned to the assistant director as mutually agreeable.

The Lecture Leader

This person prepares and delivers the lecture at the weekly assembly. **(Lesson material for the lecture leader begins on p. 8.)** The lecture leader

- prepares and presents the Bible study lecture to the large group;

- prepares worship activities (devotional thought, hymn, prayer), using resources in the study leaflet and leaders guide and possibly other, outside sources;
- helps the small-group discussion leaders to grow in understanding the content of the lessons;
- encourages prayer at weekly leadership-team and discussion-leaders meetings.

The Small-Group Coordinator *(optional; the director may fill this role)*

This person supervises and coordinates the work of the small-group discussion leaders. The small-group coordinator

- recruits with the leadership team the small-group discussion leaders;
- trains or arranges for training of the discussion leaders;
- assists the director and discussion leaders in follow-up and outreach;
- encourages the discussion leaders to contact absent group members;
- participates in the weekly leadership-team and discussion-leaders equipping meetings;
- provides ongoing training and support as needed.

The Small-Group Discussion Leaders

These people guide and facilitate discussion of LifeLight participants in the small groups. **(Lesson material for the small-group leaders begins on p. 55.)** There should be one discussion leader for every group of no more than twelve participants. The small-group discussion leaders are, perhaps, those individuals who are most important to the success of the program. They should, therefore, be chosen with special care and be equipped with skills needed to guide discussion and to foster a caring fellowship within the group. These discussion leaders

- prepare each week for the small-group discussion by using the study leaflet and small-group leaders guide section for that session **(see p. 55);**
- read the enrichment magazine as a study supplement;
- guide and facilitate discussion in their small group;
- encourage and assist the discussion group in prayer;
- foster fellowship and mutual care within the discussion group;
- attend weekly discussion-leaders training meetings.

Leadership Training

LifeLight leaders will meet weekly to review the previous week's work and plan the coming week. At this session, leaders can address concerns and prepare for the coming session. LifeLight is a 1½-hour program with no possibility for it to be taught in the one hour typically available on Sunday mornings. Some congregations, however, may want to use the Sunday morning Bible study hour for LifeLight preparation and leadership training. In such a meeting, the lecture leader and/or small-group coordinator may lead the discussion leaders through the coming week's lesson, reserving 5 or 10 minutes for problem solving or other group concerns.

While it requires intense effort, LifeLight has proven to bring great benefit to LifeLight participants. The effort put into this program, both by leaders and by participants, will be rewarding and profitable.

The LifeLight Weekly Schedule

Here is how LifeLight will work week by week:

1. Before session 1, each participant will receive the study leaflet for session 1 and the enrichment magazine for the course. The study leaflet contains worship resources (for use both in individual daily study and at the opening of the following week's assembly) and readings and study questions for five days. Challenge questions will lead those participants who have the time and who desire a greater challenge into even deeper levels of study.

2. After the five days of individual study at home, participants will gather for a weekly assembly of all LifeLight participants. The assembly will begin with a brief period of worship (5 minutes). Participants will then join their assigned small discussion groups (of twelve or fewer, who will remain the same throughout the course), where they will go over the week's study questions together (55 minutes). Assembling together once again, participants will listen to a lecture presentation on the readings they have studied in the previous week and discussed in their small groups (20 minutes). After the lecture presentation, the director or another leader will distribute the study leaflet for the following week.

Closing announcements and other necessary business may take another 5 minutes before dismissal.

In some places, some small groups will not join the weekly assembly because of scheduling or other reasons. Such groups may meet at another time and place (perhaps in the home of one of the small group's members). Those congregations may record the lecture given by the lecture leader at the weekly assembly and duplicate it for use by other groups meeting later in the week.

3. On the day following the assembly, participants will review the preceding week's work by rereading the study leaflet they completed (and that they perhaps supplemented or corrected during the discussion in their small group) and by reading appropriate articles in the enrichment magazine.

Then the LifeLight weekly study process will begin all over again!

Recommended Study Resources and Worship

The Lutheran Study Bible. St. Louis: Concordia Publishing House, 2009. This resource contains more than 26,000 study and application notes, a most thorough reference guide (pp. lxv–cx), and over 90,000 cross-references, as well as a 31,000-entry concordance, maps, charts, and timelines.

Roehrs, Walter R., and Martin H. Franzmann. *Concordia Self-Study Commentary.* St. Louis: Concordia Publishing House, 1979. This one-volume commentary on the Bible contains 950 pages and is tailored for lay use.

The Concordia Organist is a 31-CD collection of pipe organ accompaniments for all the hymns and liturgical music in *Lutheran Service Book.* St. Louis: Concordia Publishing House (order no. 99-2264). Use these CDs for worship hymn accompaniment.

The Day of the Lord Is Near
Obadiah

Preparing for the Session

Central Focus

God's power and grace are seen in His reign on behalf of His people. He brings judgment upon those—like the Edomites—who reject Him, and He restores those who are His.

Objectives

That participants, led by the Holy Spirit working through God's Word, will

1. appreciate God's rule over all the nations;
2. stand in awe of God's judgments upon unrighteousness and unbelief; and
3. humbly trust God's grace toward His people.

Note for the small-group leaders: Lesson notes and other materials you will need begin on page 55.

For the Lecture Leader

Session Plan

Worship

Begin the session with the hymn printed in the study leaflet. Accompaniments are available in denominational hymnals, such as *Lutheran Service Book* or *Lutheran Worship* (refer to hymnal index). (Note: Concordia Publishing House has available *The Concordia Organist*. All the initial worship hymns in the LifeLight courses are included in this resource. It's especially helpful for mission congregations and small parishes. See the list of study resources on p. 7.) Follow with this prayer:

Prayer

Lord God, in Your infinite wisdom and by Your almighty power, You exalt and You make small. Keep us from sinful pride and arrogance that would turn us from You, our only hope and our sure salvation. Forgive us our many sins, and renew us daily through Jesus Christ, Your Son, our Lord, who lives and reigns with You and the Holy Spirit, one God, now and forever. Amen.

Lecture Presentation

Introduction

Like each of the other nine Minor Prophets, Obadiah, Jonah, and Micah are distinctly individual in their historical circumstances, messages, and applications. For example, two of these three prophets, Obadiah and Jonah, directed their prophecies toward foreign nations, while Micah's prophetic ministry was focused on the nation of Judah. Yet, like the others, each is divinely inspired and presents God's Law—condemning sin and unbelief—and His Gospel—promising forgiveness and salvation in the coming Messiah, the Christ.

Obadiah is the shortest book in the Old Testament, only one chapter long, a mere twenty-one verses. Its powerful message, however, has proven worthy of much discussion through the centuries and continues to resound to our generation.

The name Obadiah means "servant of the Lord [Yahweh]." It is used of more than a dozen men in the Old Testament. Little is known of the Obadiah who authored the book that bears his name. Some have suggested he is the Obadiah mentioned in 2 Chronicles 17:7, who was among the officials sent out by King Jehoshaphat to revive true worship in the land and instruct the people of Judah in the Law of the Lord. The identification of the person Obadiah immediately brings up the issue of the date of the book. If the Obadiah just mentioned was the author of the book, he would most likely be the earliest of the literary prophets, carrying on his ministry about 850 years before Christ.

Most commentators, including Martin Luther, have opted for a much later date, which would put Obadiah and his prophecy around the time of the fall of Jerusalem to the Babylonians in 587 BC. Although other commentators would date the book even later—about 400 BC—the dates of 845 and 587 are the two most likely.

The large discrepancy in dating relates to Obadiah's mention of the fall of Jerusalem in verse 11. Most see this as the conquest by the Babylonians. There was, however, an earlier incident in which the Philistines and Arabians plundered Jerusalem, during the reign of King Jehoram (853–841), as recorded in 2 Chronicles 21:16–17 (see also 2 Kings 8:20). In either case, the Lord says to the

Edomites, on that day "you stood aloof" (Obadiah 11). Beyond that, they rejoiced in the despoiling of Jerusalem. Psalm 137:7 relates this to the Babylonian destruction, but given the centuries-old hatred of Edom toward Jerusalem, this does not rule out their doing it at an earlier time as well.

On behalf of the earlier date is the fact that the prophecy of Obadiah is placed among the earlier prophets, and it contains no mention of the total destruction of the temple that took place at the hands of the Babylonians. As we shall see, Jeremiah 49:7–22 strongly parallels the first eleven verses of Obadiah; it is likely that Jeremiah borrowed from the earlier prophecy, just as he did from the prophets Isaiah and Amos who lived before him. Moreover, the book's brevity seems fitting as the earliest venture into literary prophecy. (While leaning toward this option, this writer is aware of the case made for either side.) The dating changes neither the message nor the people of whom it speaks.

For the most part, Obadiah's message is directed to and against Edom, a nation located to the southeast of the Dead Sea (also known as the Salt Sea) and to the east of the Great Rift or Wadi Arabah Valley, which extends 100 miles south from the Dead Sea to the Gulf of Aqaba. Protected by desert mountains between 4,000 and 5,000 feet in height and by deep, forbidding gorges, the land was all but impregnable. From lofty heights, the Edomites, like eagles, could destroy and prey upon those who dared to pass below. Through Edom ran the King's Highway, from Damascus in the north to the Gulf of Aqaba in the south, where caravans could turn west toward Egypt or east toward Arabia and beyond.

When Moses and the Israelites came from Egypt and requested to pass through Edom on their way to the Promised Land, they were refused and instead had to journey about a hundred miles out of their way through harsh, arid lands (Numbers 20:14–21). (Today the impressive ruins of Petra—the city carved into the sandstone cliffs of Edom some time later—remain as one of the most awesome sites in the entire Middle East.)

The hard feelings between Edom and Israel went back into the even more distant past than the time of Moses. The name Edom is a variant from the name Esau, both of which are related to the meaning "red," as in the red clay or dirt of the land. The people were descendants of Esau, the older twin brother of Jacob, who later became known as Israel. Esau harbored deep feelings of resentment toward Israel, who, instead of Esau, received the blessing from their father, Isaac. Esau had brought this on himself by his disregard for the blessings that would have been his as the elder of the two brothers.

Although the brothers were eventually reconciled, the subsequent history of their descendants was one of frequent hostility. Because of Edom's mistreatment of the descendants of Israel, Obadiah predicted doom for the nation of Edom. Eventually, in the first century after Christ, the remnant of Edom was assimilated into the various peoples of the region and lost their national identity.

The history of the relatively small nation of Edom, then, is an account of one nation's pride bringing about its fall. It is representative of all resentment against God's plans and against His people, and of God's eventual judgment against those who oppose His will.

1 Introduction: The Vision of Obadiah *(1a)*

"The vision of . . ."—or variations thereof—is a common introduction to the books of the Old Testament prophets. We find the same terminology at the beginning of the Book of Isaiah. The prophets Nahum, Habakkuk, and Malachi use a different word, "oracle." Hosea, Joel, Jonah, Micah, Zephaniah, Haggai, and Zechariah open their prophetic books with "The word of the LORD that came to Hosea [Joel, Jonah, etc.]"; and Jeremiah and Amos begin with "The words of Jeremiah [Amos]."

Such introductory expressions set the tone for the prophetic books. The prophets spoke words that the Lord inspired them to write. Looking back from the vantage point of the New Testament, the apostle Peter wrote, (2 Peter 1:21) "For no prophecy was ever produced by the will of man, but men spoke from God as they were carried along by the Holy Spirit."

The prophets spoke in the name of the Lord and by His directive. Moreover, guided by the Holy Spirit, what they wrote was inerrant. When we think of prophets, we tend to think immediately in terms of telling the future, and that was certainly the case at times. When they did speak in the Lord's name of future events, everything they said would come to pass. In the Book of Deuteronomy, God through Moses distinguished true from false prophets: (18:21–22) "And if you [the people] say in your heart, 'How may we know the word that the LORD has not spoken?'—when a prophet speaks in the name of the LORD, if the word does not come to pass or come true, that is a word that the LORD has not spoken; the prophet has spoken it presumptuously. You need not be afraid of him.' "

Moreover, much of the prophetic material of the Old Testament Scriptures was not looking to the future but was dealing with issues contemporaneous to their own times. They were the preachers of their days; in fact, the Scriptures mention groups or schools of prophets (see, for example, 1 Samuel 19:18–24), although they must have been quite different than our modern-day seminaries for the training of pastors. In speaking of their own times or of the future, the inspired prophets were always accurate—for they were the spokesmen for God Himself.

2 Edom Will Be Humbled *(1b–9)*

The text of Obadiah is divided between speeches of the Lord and of the prophet. God's speeches take up verses 2–4, 8–18; Obadiah's speeches cover verses 5–7, 19–21. The sections in which God speaks directly are almost exactly twice the length of the prophet's.

This section opens with "Thus says the Lord God concerning Edom." Expressions such as "thus says the Lord" or "the word of the Lord came" occur more than 2,400 times in the Old Testament, with over half of those occurrences in the writings of the prophets.

Here, the Lord calls on the nations to rise up against Edom. Often throughout history, God has used nations to punish others for their wickedness. Notable examples are His use of wicked Babylon to bring down Judah for its idolatry, and then, in turn, using mighty Persia to bring down Babylon.

The Lord gets to the heart of Edom's sin that calls for her destruction: "the pride of your heart" (v. 3). Secure in her position "in the clefts of the rock, in your lofty dwelling," Edom felt she was invincible. No matter how sure people or nations might feel because of their strategic position, wealth, military might, wisdom, or other resources, the almighty God says to the arrogant, "I will bring you down."

Pride is a sin against which Scripture speaks most forcefully, for this sin sets oneself against God and looks to the self rather than the Creator and Savior. Moreover, from pride come a host of other evils: hatred, murder, thievery, and so on. God challenged Job, (Job 40:12) "Look on everyone who is proud and bring him low and tread down the wicked where they stand." And the Lord does bring them low.

Obadiah uses the name Esau as synonymous with Edom, since as mentioned above, the Edomites were descendants of Esau. The name Edom means "red," and the red (or rose-colored) sandstone cliffs among which the Edomites lived reflected the name and its meaning. In speaking of Esau's descendants in Genesis 36, the text says that Esau settled in the land that would bear his name. It goes on to mention a grandson by the name of Teman.

One of Edom's two major cities took the name Teman (the other chief city and capital was Bozrah). Through Obadiah, the Lord warns, (v. 9) "Your mighty men shall be dismayed, O Teman."

Teman was also the hometown of one of Job's three friends, Eliphaz (Job 2:11). It is striking that in arguing with Job, Eliphaz assumed a wisdom that he did not really have, and at the end of the Book of Job, God reproved him: (42:7) "the Lord said to Eliphaz the Temanite: 'My anger burns against you and against your two friends, for you have not spoken of Me what is right, as My servant Job has.'" In Obadiah, God declares, (v. 8) "Will I not . . . destroy the wise men out of Edom?" Edom's wisdom, like its vaunted sense of security, proved to be empty.

The opening nine verses of Obadiah contain strong parallels with the prophet Jeremiah (ch. 49). A few examples will elucidate this:

> Obadiah 1: "We have heard a report from the Lord, and a messenger has been sent among the nations."
> Jeremiah 49:14: "I have heard a message from the Lord, and an envoy has been sent among the nations." (In the Hebrew original, "report" and "message" are the same word, as are "messenger" and "envoy.")
>
> Obadiah 2: "I will make you small among the nations; you shall be utterly despised."
> Jeremiah 49:15: "I will make you small among the nations, despised among mankind."
>
> Obadiah 4: "Though you soar aloft like the eagle, though your nest is set among the stars, from there I will bring you down, declares the Lord."
> Jeremiah 49:16: "Though you make your nest as high as the eagle's, I will bring you down from there, declares the Lord."

Readers may wish to compare the sections more thoroughly.

We will make note of another such similarity in our study of Micah—between Micah 4:15 and Isaiah 2:1–5—and comment more on this phenomenon at that point. Such interconnectedness is but one of many features of Scripture that point to its marvelous unity.

Although comprised of sixty-six separate books, the Bible is one book (the word *Bible* means "book"). Unified in message and purpose, the separate books overlap and reinforce one another, with all of them depicting the themes of sin and grace, judgment and salvation in Christ.

3 Edom's Violence against Jacob *(10–14)*

The Lord closely connects Edom with Esau: (Obadiah 10) "Because of the violence done to your brother Jacob, shame shall cover you." Esau had wanted to kill his brother Jacob, who had to flee for his life. Throughout subsequent centuries, the animosity continued with the descendants of Esau holding an unending grudge against their relatives, the children of Israel (Jacob). In the world of today, we see a similar phenomenon in the animosity between Arabs and Jews—with both people tracing their origins back to Abraham (the Jewish people through his son Isaac, and the Arab people through his son Ishmael). While this goes beyond the scope of biblical interpretation, it is a reminder that people can be at odds for centuries.

In the case of the Edomites, their anger against their blood relatives, the people of Israel, was ultimately against God. The children of Israel were the chosen people, bearers of the promise of the Messiah, the Christ, who would be the Savior of the human race. The central verse of Obadiah (v. 11) expresses the culmination of this hatred: "On the day that you stood aloof, on the day that strangers carried off his wealth and foreigners entered his gates and cast lots for Jerusalem, you were like one of them."

In Hebrew literature, the central verse of a book or portion of a book may be a climatic point. We see this in the Book of Job, where in the center of Job's discourses with his friends, he makes his monumental statement of faith: "I know that my Redeemer lives" (Job 19:25). In the central verses of the Song of Solomon, we find the culmination of the love between the man and woman: She says, "Let my beloved come to his garden," and he responds, "I came to my garden" (4:16–5:1). And in the center of the second half of the Book of Isaiah, we find the magnificent chapter on the Suffering Servant of the Lord—one of the most detailed prophecies of the Christ (Isaiah 52:12–53:12).

In the Obadiah passage, we see the Edomites standing aloof and then even participating in the pillaging of Jerusalem, where the temple of the Lord God stood on Mount Moriah. Instead of coming to its aid, the Edomites entered Jerusalem to loot it. The expression "cast lots" refers to the dividing of the spoils, and it reminds us how at Jesus' crucifixion the soldiers cast lots for His robe (John 19:24, in fulfillment of Psalm 22:18). Exactly what was involved in the casting of lots is not certain. Some have suggested that people would remove marked sticks or pebbles from a container into which they had been cast. Whatever the method, the Edomites were using the practice to take part with the enemies of God's people in dividing the spoils. The Lord warns them, (v. 12) "Do not gloat . . . do not rejoice . . . do not boast." The day of reckoning would come for the people of Edom. What a warning to all who proudly mock God, His messengers, and His faithful people!

4 The Day of the Lord Is Near *(15–18)*

"The day of the Lord is near." Through His prophet Obadiah, God uses this expression or variants thereof a number of times. It is frequently used in the prophets and refers to that time when God will intervene in history. It often is depicted as a day of terrible judgment upon sin and unbelief, as the prophet Joel says, (2:11) "For the day of the Lord is great and very awesome; who can endure it?" It can also be a time of comfort for believers, as Joel says elsewhere, (3:18) "And in that day the mountains shall drip sweet wine."

The New Testament uses expressions such as "the day of Jesus Christ" or "the day of Christ" (Philippians 1:6, 10). This, of course, refers to the day when Christ will return—that is the ultimate and consummate day of the Lord, a day of dread for unbelievers and a day of rejoicing for those who await His coming.

For Edom and all the nations of the world, there is a day that marks their end. Edom met its end already. All will come to an end on Judgment Day. It is always "near" and can come at any time.

Mount Zion (Obadiah 17) is a hill in Jerusalem, often used to represent the entire city, with the temple of the Lord. Jerusalem in turn has come to represent God's people. There, says the Lord, is escape from danger, "and it shall be holy." Edom would eventually be swallowed up by Jacob and his descendants—represented here by Joseph.

In subsequent history, Obadiah's prophecy concerning Edom unfolded. Edom was overrun by the Babylonian armies of Nebuchadnezzar's son Nabonidus around 553/2 BC. A little more than a century after that, the

Arab tribe of Nabataeans drove the Edomites out and built what are now the ruins of Petra. After the conquest of Alexander the Great spread the Greek language, Edom became known as Idumea (a term later used in the New Testament). The Jewish leader Judas Maccabeus defeated them in 185 BC; some time later, Judaism was forced on them. The most famous of the Idumeans was King Herod the Great, who rose to power under the Romans and is notorious for his slaughter of the babies of Bethlehem shortly after Jesus was born.

When the Jews revolted against Rome in AD 70, the Idumeans sided with the Jews and were put down. What few survivors remained were absorbed into the people around them. As God had said through Obadiah: (v. 18) "There shall be no survivor for the house of Esau, for the LORD has spoken."

5 The Kingdom of the Lord *(19–21)*

The closing words of Obadiah are uplifting for God's people. He says people will come from the Negeb (south of Judah) to "possess" Mount Esau and from the Shephelah (Judean foothills) to "possess" the land of the Philistines, and so on; the word "possess" occurs six times here. In other words, God's people will occupy the land. Some ancient rabbis identified Sepharad (v. 20; which is used only here in all of Scripture) as Spain; the label Sephardic Jew (Spanish Jew) derives from this understanding. More likely, it refers to a site somewhere in the eastern Mediterranean world, possibly in Asia Minor, Greece, or even Assyria.

Although ancient Jewish rabbis tended to see this text as designating Jerusalem as the gathering place for all nations, early Christian interpreters such as St. Augustine (354–430) and subsequent commentators have found its fulfillment in the Messiah, Jesus Christ. Martin Luther, for example, pointed out that a literal, physical interpretation would contradict Old Testament law, which did not allow for the re-division of the land. Instead of a physical fulfillment, then, the completion of the prophecy is spiritual and points to heaven.

Although Edom—and all unbelievers—meet their day of judgment, (v. 21) "Saviors shall go up to Mount Zion to rule Mount Esau, and the kingdom shall be the LORD's." The word "saviors" can also be translated "deliverers." These are the messengers who bring the good news of salvation—the Gospel—to the nations.

They will "rule" or "judge" (it is the word used of the God-appointed leaders in the Book of Judges). The kingdom is the Lord's. This is the kingdom that God has established through His Son, Jesus. It is not a kingdom of this world but one that lasts forever. This is the kingdom of which we, by God's grace, are a part.

Conclusion

Obadiah is a short book, and Edom was a relatively minor player among the nations of the ancient world. Yet the book and the message are a microcosm of so much more. Obadiah encapsulates God's dealing with all the nations throughout history. The Book of Proverbs sums it up even more succinctly, in a single verse: (14:34) "Righteousness exalts a nation, but sin is a reproach to any people."

God brings down the haughty and hardened—whether it be individuals or entire countries. What a warning this is in our own day as we see our great nation so stubbornly turn from even the most basic moral principles that had been such a part of her gloried past. (Proverbs 16:18) "Pride goes before destruction, and a haughty spirit before a fall." Like any other, our civilization is not immune to the judgment of God.

Obadiah is also a reminder that amid the most tumultuous and troubled times, God is with His people. He will never leave us nor forsake us. Although the mountains fall into the heart of the sea, God is with His people.

Concluding Activities

Conclude the session with an appropriate prayer and distribute the study leaflet for week 2.

Arise, Go to Nineveh

Jonah 1

Preparing for the Session

Central Focus

God is everywhere. It is foolish to try to flee from Him. Rather than running from the Lord, we can find comfort in knowing that He is always there for His people.

Objectives

That participants, led by the Holy Spirit working through God's Word, will

1. accept their roles as workers in God's kingdom;
2. follow God's guidance in their lives; and
3. recognize the need for regular study of the Scriptures.

Note for the small-group leaders: Lesson notes and other materials you will need begin on page 57.

For the Lecture Leader

Session Plan

Worship

Begin the session with the hymn printed in the study leaflet. Accompaniments are available in denominational hymnals, such as *Lutheran Service Book* or *Lutheran Worship* (refer to hymnal index). (Note: Concordia Publishing House has available *The Concordia Organist*. All the initial worship hymns in the LifeLight courses are included in this resource. It's especially helpful for mission congregations and small parishes. See the list of study resources on p. 7.) Follow with this prayer:

Prayer

O Lord, salvation belongs to You, and You alone! You have given us the Great Commission to preach the Gospel to all nations. How often we, like Jonah, have wanted to flee rather than to serve. Forgive us our indifference, cowardice, and prejudice. Embolden us by Your Spirit, through Jesus Christ, Your Son, our Lord, who lives and reigns with You and the Holy Spirit, one God, now and forever. Amen.

Lecture Presentation

Introduction

Jonah stands as one of the earlier of the Minor Prophets, close in time to Elijah and his successor Elisha, two of the greatest Old Testament prophets. Although their actions and words are recorded in the Scriptures, they themselves were not literary prophets. That is, they did not put their prophecies into writing. Coming shortly after their time, Jonah was like them in that the book bearing his name may well have not been written by him. Rather, it is about him. Although tradition has ascribed the book to Jonah himself, it is written in the third-person (he) rather than the first-person voice (I). Because of strong similarities to the histories of Elijah and Elisha, some have suggested that it came from the same line of sources that wrote their accounts. Whether written by Jonah or not, the book stands outside the other literary prophets. One may conclude that, rather than being a book *by* him, Jonah is a book *about* him.

The name Jonah means "dove," and it has been pointed out that Jonah had a passive (dovelike) nature. He did not want to confront the people of Nineveh; on the ship, he invited the others to throw him overboard; he was ready to die when things did not go his way. Yet he also had a willful, stubborn nature, and he was willing to try to escape the call of God Almighty. In the various aspects of his personality, Jonah showed himself to be complex, conflicted, and, yes, very human. Although he was a prophet, Jonah—like other great figures in the Bible, except Jesus Christ—was a sinful human being in need of God's love and forgiveness.

Jonah has been called the unwilling missionary. But he wasn't the first one, nor would he be the last. Centuries earlier, Moses had offered excuses not to return to Egypt to lead the people of Israel from their captivity (Exodus 3). A century and a half after Jonah, in response to God's calling, Jeremiah pleaded, "Ah, Lord GOD! Behold, I do not know how to speak, for I am only a youth" (Jeremiah 1:6). And today, we are often all too ready to explain why we cannot do this or that for the Lord.

Because of the miraculous story of Jonah in the belly of the great fish (contrary to popular notions, the Bible does not say "whale"), many modern readers are skeptical concerning the historicity of the Book of Jonah. Did it really happen? As we'll see in our exposition of the book, Jesus took it as real history. For Christians, that should be enough.

During Jonah's lifetime, the superpower of the ancient world was Assyria, with its capital of Nineveh. Located on the eastern bank of the Tigris River in the northern part of what is modern-day Iraq, Nineveh was a spectacular city, with gateways lined by huge statues—weighing thirty or forty tons!—of winged bulls with human heads and lion sphinxes, aqueducts to bring fresh water from the mountains, and a magnificent library, in which archaeologists have found over 25,000 clay tablets attesting to the glory of Nineveh and the Assyrian Empire.

But Nineveh was an idolatrous city, given to the worship of many gods and goddesses, thousands of them for every force of nature and every human activity: a moon god, a sun god, a god for the weather, another for carpenters, and even one for brewers. In the temples were statues of the idols, made of wood or stone and covered with precious metals. Magicians served in the temples and palaces, as did astrologers and fortune-tellers.

Today the ruins of Nineveh lie across the river from Mosul, the second largest city of Iraq (Baghdad being the largest) and the capital of the governorate or province of Ninawa (Nineveh).

As we shall see, Jonah despised this empire with its idols and its arrogance. Nevertheless, after he reluctantly preached God's words of warning to Nineveh, the city repented and was spared. Almost two centuries later, Nineveh was beyond repentance and was destroyed by the Babylonians, as foretold by the prophet Nahum.

1 Jonah's Commission *(1:1–2)*

"Now the word of the Lord came to Jonah the son of Amittai." The father's name means "loyal" or "faithful." In the end, although Jonah did God's bidding, it was, as will become evident, reluctantly and with reservations.

How did God convey His Word to the prophets? Sometimes in a vision, as that of Isaiah in the temple in Jerusalem (Isaiah 6); sometimes in words heard in the physical ears, as to Isaiah (Isaiah 22:14); sometimes in a whisper, as to Elijah (1 Kings 19:12); sometimes accompanied by music, as with Elisha (2 Kings 3:15). Often, as with Jonah, we are not told.

He was called to go to Nineveh, the great capital of the Assyrian Empire, located more than 500 miles northeast of Jonah's home. There, he was to preach God's judgment against the sins of the people of Nineveh. Most of the prophets of the Old Testament preached to their own people—the inhabitants of Israel and Judah. Some spoke about the surrounding nations and beyond. Yet Jonah was to go and preach to this foreign city.

2 Jonah Flees from the Presence of the Lord *(1:3–6)*

In 1 Kings 17:2 and elsewhere, it is written that "the word of the Lord came to" the prophet Elijah, one of the most illustrious characters in the entire Old Testament. Here the same expression is used in regard to the prophet Jonah. Although the initial calling was the same in both cases, the reaction was markedly different.

Of Elijah it is said, "he went" as God directed him. Elijah boldly declared to wicked King Ahab, "As the Lord, the God of Israel, lives, before whom I stand" (1 Kings 17:1; literally, he says "in His [God's] presence"). Of Jonah, we read that he "rose to flee to Tarshish from the presence of the Lord." While other prophets may have been reluctant (Moses and Jeremiah), and at times became discouraged (Elijah), none of them went so far as to disobey God's calling, as did Jonah.

Instead of heading to Nineveh, which lay to the northeast of the Holy Land, Jonah went to the Mediterranean seaport city of Joppa and boarded a ship that would take him in the opposite direction—to Tarshish. Located thirty-five miles northwest of Jerusalem, Joppa, or Jaffa (modern-day Yafo), in New Testament times witnessed the restoring to life of Tabitha (Dorcas; Acts 9) and Peter's vision that the Gospel was to be preached to the Gentiles (Acts 10). Ironically, Jonah tried to use Joppa as a place to run away from preaching to the Gentiles. The location of Tarshish is uncertain. Tarsus in Asia Minor (modern-day Turkey) is one possibility; another is much more distant Spain, which lay at the opposite end of the Great Sea; that is, the Mediterranean.

As will almost immediately become evident, Jonah's attempt to flee from God was foolish. God is omnipresent—everywhere present—and it is not possible to flee from Him. The psalmist David had proclaimed this before Jonah's time: (Psalm 139:7–12)

> Where shall I go from Your Spirit?
> Or where shall I flee from Your presence?
> If I ascend to heaven, You are there!
> If I make my bed in Sheol, You are there!
> If I take the wings of the morning
> and dwell in the uttermost parts of the sea,
> even there Your hand shall lead me,
> and Your right hand shall hold me.

> If I say, "Surely the darkness shall cover me,
> and the light about me be night,"
> even the darkness is not dark to You;
> the night is bright as the day,
> for darkness is as light with You.

The impossibility of fleeing from God is a source of terror to all who would defy Him and His will. It is a source of comfort to those who daily call to Him for help and strength. The term Sheol—the place of the dead—that David uses, will also find its way into the psalm prayer that Jonah will later offer (Jonah 2:2).

The Lord was not about to let Jonah run away. (1:4) "The Lord hurled a great wind upon the sea, and there was a mighty tempest." In spite of the storm that was threatening to destroy the ship, Jonah was inside, "fast asleep." The captain came and said to the prophet, "Arise, call out to your god!" The storm, the slumber, and the calling for divine deliverance are striking as they parallel an event that would transpire centuries later. The Gospels record how a storm arose on the Sea of Galilee when Jesus and His disciples were in a boat: (Mark 4:37–38)

> And a great windstorm arose, and the waves were breaking into the boat, so that the boat was already filling. But [Jesus] was in the stern, asleep on the cushion. And they woke Him and said to Him, "Teacher, do You not care that we are perishing?"

3 Jonah Is Thrown into the Sea *(1:7–16)*

As the storm raged, the sailors "cast lots" to discover "on whose account this evil" had come upon them. As we have noted in our study of Obadiah, the casting of lots was a common custom among the ancients. In this case, the lots pointed to Jonah as the one responsible for the disaster that had descended upon them.

Despite Jonah's reluctance to carry out God's call, he knew that the Lord was behind this storm. He told the crew, (v. 9) "I am a Hebrew, and I fear the Lord, the God of heaven, who made the sea and the dry land." The term "Hebrew" goes back to the name Eber (Genesis 10:24), who was one of the ancestors of Abraham from whom the people of Israel had descended. Jonah then told the men that because he had brought about this disaster, if they threw him overboard, the sea would "quiet down." No sooner had the men throw Jonah into the sea then "the sea ceased from its raging." Overawed by what had just transpired, "the men feared the Lord exceedingly, and they offered a sacrifice to the Lord." How ironic that even when he had tried to run away from his mission, Jonah turned out to be a missionary!

To return to the strikingly parallel account in the Gospels: (Mark 4:39–41)

> And [Jesus] awoke and rebuked the wind and said to the sea, "Peace! Be still!" And the wind ceased, and there was a great calm. He said to them, "Why are you so afraid? Have you still no faith?" And they were filled with great fear and said to one another, "Who then is this, that even the wind and the sea obey Him?"

The ruler of wind and wave, who calmed the sea at Jonah's time, later experienced a storm from Jonah's point of view. And once again He showed His power over His own creation. Another even more remarkable parallel between the prophet Jonah and Christ is soon to unfold—that of their deliverance from death.

The Bible also records another storm on the Mediterranean. Luke, the writer of the Book of Acts, gives a vivid description of that tempest involving himself, the apostle Paul, and a total of 276 on board: (Acts 27:13–20)

> Now when the south wind blew gently, supposing that they had obtained their purpose, they weighed anchor and sailed along Crete, close to the shore. But soon a tempestuous wind, called the northeaster, struck down from the land. And when the ship was caught and could not face the wind, we gave way to it and were driven along. . . . Since we were violently storm-tossed, they began the next day to jettison the cargo. . . . When neither sun nor stars appeared for many days, and no small tempest lay on us, all hope of our being saved was at last abandoned.

Although the storm ended in shipwreck, all onboard were brought safely to land on the island of Malta.

In each of these storms on the water, God was in charge of the forces of nature, and each case ended in safety for those involved. When storms come into our lives—whether at sea or figuratively—the Lord will see us through them. God is the all-powerful ruler of wind and wave; as Psalm 89:9 puts it, "You rule the raging of the sea; when its waves rise, You calm them."

It is ironic that even though Jonah tried to run from his commission, he ended up preaching to the sailors. God used Jonah's few words to turn their hearts so that they "feared the Lord" (this can also be translated "worshiped" or "trusted"), offered a sacrifice, and made vows. In other words, they were brought to faith.

Meanwhile, as the storm was breaking up and the sun was breaking through the clouds, Jonah was sinking down into the depths of the Mediterranean Sea. Perhaps he was able to observe a bubbly glimmer of light above his head as he descended into the watery darkness below.

4 A Great Fish Swallows Jonah *(1:17)*

In the original text of the Hebrew Old Testament and the Greek New Testament Scriptures, there were no chapter and verse designations. Stephen Langton (1150–1228), a professor at the University of Paris and later the Archbishop of Canterbury, is credited with dividing the Bible into the chapter divisions we use today. Later, a Parisian printer, Robert Stephanus (1503–50), further divided the chapters into verse designations. Such divisions are very helpful for locating passages in the Bible, for readings in church services, for cross referencing, and for many other uses.

Occasionally, the placement of a chapter break is of interest in discussing the actual content of the various passages. For example, the break from the six days of creation and God resting on the seventh day actually occurs after Genesis 2:3, not at the end of Genesis 1. In regard to Jonah, Hebrew editions of the Bible include Jonah 1:17 with the following chapter. In that scenario, chapter 2 opens with Jonah being swallowed by the fish and ends with him being vomited out of the fish, with those two verses serving like bookends for his prayer from within the fish for deliverance.

This point helps us better understand the structure of the book. Until Jonah is swallowed by the fish, the Book of Jonah is all about the prophet's fleeing from his God-given commission. After he is delivered from the great fish, the book is all about his fulfilling the commission, be it ever so grudgingly.

But what of this "great fish"? Although commonly referred to as a whale, that is not specifically stated in the Bible's original Hebrew text, which simply uses the generic word for fish (*dag*). There are stories of sailors who were swallowed by fish and lived to tell about it, one as recently as 1987 (see R. Reed Lessing, *Jonah*, Concordia Commentary Series [St. Louis: Concordia Publishing House, 2007], 187). This was of course, no mere lucky occurrence for Jonah. God was working a miracle that would both save His prophet and foreshadow His Son's resurrection from the dead.

5 Jonah and Christ

Centuries after Jonah's time, Jesus likened Himself to Jonah: (Matthew 12:40)

> For just as Jonah was three days and three nights in the belly of the great fish, so will the Son of Man be three days and three nights in the heart of the earth.

The three days and three nights are at first glance perplexing. After all, Jesus wasn't in the tomb for three nights. According to the Jewish manner of speaking, any part of a day was considered part of a complete day. This is evident from the Book of Esther, when Queen Esther said, (4:16) "Go, gather all the Jews to be found in Susa, and hold a fast on my behalf, and do not eat or drink for three days, night or day. . . . Then I will go to the king." Later we are told, (5:1) "On the third day Esther put on her royal robes and stood in the inner court of the king's palace, in front of the king's quarters, while the king was sitting on his royal throne." Although three complete days and nights had not yet passed, Esther had kept her word.

We will return to our discussion of the connection between Jonah's time in the fish and Jesus' time in the tomb in the next section. For now, however, we will spend a moment on the idea of Jonah as a "type" of Christ. An Old Testament type is different from a direct prophecy, which overtly states some feature of the coming Messiah or messianic age. For example, Isaiah foretold the coming of the God-man: (9:6) "For to us a child is born, to us a son is given; . . . and His name shall be called Wonderful Counselor, Mighty God."

Rather than setting forth such direct proclamations, a type paints a picture, the image of which corresponds to a feature of Christ. For example, Jesus Himself alluded to the bronze serpent in the wilderness (Numbers 21:4–9) as a type of Himself: (John 3:14–16) "And as Moses lifted up the serpent in the wilderness, so must the Son of Man be lifted up, that whoever believes in Him may have eternal life. For God so loved the world, that He gave His only Son, that whoever believes in Him should not perish but have eternal life." Another type of Christ was the Passover lamb. As the lamb's blood was shed to deliver the people from death, Christ is the "Lamb of God," whose blood washes away the sins of the world. Of course, people would not have known that any given historical event would prefigure Christ, but the pattern or image was there and the mind was attuned to God's working out of His plan of salvation.

The other aspect of typology is the anti-type. Scripture contrasts the first man, the first Adam, with Jesus, the last Adam (1 Corinthians 15:45). Just as the first man brought sin and death into the world, the second Adam has brought forgiveness and life: (Romans 5:19) "For as by the one man's disobedience the many were made sinners, so by the one man's obedience the many will be made righteous." As Jonah could be said to be a type of Christ in some ways, in other ways he, like Adam, was an anti-type—presenting an opposite image. Jonah fled from God's commission; Jesus said, "Your will be done" (Matthew 26:42). Jonah was helpless in the storm; Jesus calmed the storm.

As we read the Bible, we need to be careful not to see these types where they are not warranted but let the New Testament guide us in identifying them. That being said, and without reading too much into Old Testament texts, we also need to remember that all the Scriptures testify to Jesus, as He Himself asserts. Speaking to His contemporaries about the Old Testament Scriptures, He said, (John 5:39) "You search the Scriptures because you think that in them you have eternal life; and it is they that bear witness about Me." Jonah, then, in some ways was a type of Christ, prefiguring the coming Messiah.

Conclusion

Jonah was undeniably the reluctant missionary. Yet if we take a look at ourselves, we can see much of Jonah in our lives as well. How often we would rather go in the opposite direction—doing anything but taking the opportunities that God places before us!

In our study of Jonah, we have noted a number of parallels between Jonah and Christ—some shedding light on Jonah as a type of Christ, others as an anti-type or contrast. It is also of value to compare and contrast Jonah with Obadiah. In common, both were called to proclaim God's Word to foreign nations outside the chosen nation of Israel. From what we know, Obadiah willingly accepted that call; Jonah balked at it and tried to run away. The outcome of their preaching also was in stark contrast. Edom was recalcitrant in its opposition to God and His chosen people. In its hardness of heart, Edom called down upon itself destruction. Nineveh, on the other hand, repented, and God spared the city. Its hardening of heart and destruction would wait until another, later generation.

God's Word, then, meets with one of two responses. People either believe it or reject it. There is no in-between. Jesus states, (Matthew 12:30) "Whoever is not with Me is against Me." That remains the case today. The preaching—as well as the preachers—of God's Word is, as St. Paul put it, a scent of life and death: (2 Corinthians 2:15–16) "For we are the aroma of Christ to God among those who are being saved and among those who are perishing, to one a fragrance from death to death, to the other a fragrance from life to life."

Concluding Activities

Conclude the session with an appropriate prayer and distribute the study leaflet for week 3.

Jonah's Prayer and Preaching
Jonah 2–3

Preparing for the Session

Central Focus

At any time of the day or night, even in seemingly impossible circumstances, the Lord, who neither slumbers nor sleeps, is ready and willing to hear our prayers and deliver us in our needs.

Objectives

That participants, led by the Holy Spirit working through God's Word, will

1. be strengthened in their prayer life;
2. believe the Bible's accounts of the miracles of Jonah in the fish and Christ resurrected from the grave; and
3. appreciate the power of the Word to change people's hearts.

Note for the small-group leaders: Lesson notes and other materials you will need begin on page 59.

For the Lecture Leader

Session Plan

Worship

Begin the session with the hymn printed in the study leaflet. Accompaniments are available in denominational hymnals, such as *Lutheran Service Book* or *Lutheran Worship* (refer to hymnal index). (Note: Concordia Publishing House has available *The Concordia Organist*. All the initial worship hymns in the LifeLight courses are included in this resource. It's especially helpful for mission congregations and small parishes. See the list of study resources on p. 7.) Follow with this prayer:

Prayer

O Lord our God, in our distress, we have called to You, and You have heard and answered us. Thank You for preserving our life through many dangers and for keeping us in the saving faith. Be with us until life's end, when we shall rise from death to life eternal, through Jesus, Your Son, our Lord, who lives and reigns with You and the Holy Spirit, one God, now and forever. Amen.

Lecture Presentation

Introduction

The Book of Jonah is a narrative, a story. Although Jonah 2 is part of that narrative, it is written in a different way.

For the most part, Jonah 2 is the prophet's prayer from the belly of the fish. This prayer also differs from the rest of the book in that it is in poetic format, and Jonah's words are in the first person—"I called," and so on. Because of these three features—prayer, poetry, and first person—this chapter marks a break from the narrative of the rest of Jonah.

In addition to its different literary form, the prayer is also distinctive in its tone. Jonah eagerly speaks with confidence that God will deliver him, and he thanks Him for doing so, whereas in the rest of the book, he is pessimistic toward the idea of God helping others—that is, those outside the chosen people. When it comes to Jonah's attitude toward them, he is neither eager for their deliverance nor thankful when it comes.

1 Jonah's Prayer
(2:1–9)

Jonah's prayer is poetry, like the Psalms. The distinctive feature of Hebrew poetry is parallelism, with one line running parallel to the next by presenting either the same idea (synonymous), a contrasting idea (antithetic), or an expansion on the idea (synthetic). For instance, the opening lines of the prayer state, "I called out to the Lord, out of my distress, and He answered me; out of the belly of Sheol I cried, and You heard my voice." Here, in parallel expressions that are synonymous, Jonah speaks of God's delivering him.

The Hebrew term *Sheol* is the word for the place of the dead; in the belly of the fish, Jonah was all but dead—or so it seemed. *Sheol* occurs over sixty times in the Old Testament. Occasionally, when it refers to the end of the wicked, it can mean hell. For example, the King James Version of the Bible often translates it that way, as in Psalm 9:17: "The wicked shall be turned into hell, and all the nations that forget God." At other times, the word refers to the place of the dead in general, what we would call the grave; in Psalm 16:10, David states, "You will not abandon my soul to Sheol, or let your holy one see corruption." This is a messianic psalm referring to Christ's brief stay in the tomb (see Acts 2:31); it is also an assurance of the resurrection to all believers.

From the belly of the fish, Jonah expresses to God the assurance that he will (v. 4) "again look upon your holy temple." The reference is to the temple in Jerusalem, the center of worship in ancient Israel. A few lines later, Jonah says, (v. 7) "My prayer came to You, into Your holy temple." This most likely alludes to the heavens.

At the dedication of the temple, in King Solomon's marvelous dedicatory prayer, he had recognized God's presence in both places: (1 Kings 8:38–39)

> Whatever prayer, whatever plea is made by any man or by all Your people Israel, each knowing the affliction of his own heart and stretching out his hands toward this house, then hear in heaven Your dwelling place and forgive and act and render to each whose heart You know, according to all his ways (for You, You only, know the hearts of all the children of mankind).

Earlier in that prayer, Solomon had said, (1 Kings 8:27)

> But will God indeed dwell on the earth? Behold, heaven and the highest heaven cannot contain you; how much less this house that I have built!

So no matter where we are, God hears our prayers. Our risen and ascended Savior promises, (Matthew 28:20) "I am with you always." The almighty Lord is omnipresent, with us everywhere and with us always.

In the closing two verses of Jonah's psalm-prayer, he contrasts the worship of "vain idols" with his worship of the Lord. Idolaters "forsake their hope of [God's] steadfast love," for "salvation belongs to the Lord!" The ancients worshiped idols made of wood or precious metals (for a powerful description of this, see Jeremiah 10). These idols were "vain"—empty and helpless—because they were man-made and had no power to do anything.

Modern "enlightened" people might look back on ancient idolatry with a sense of superiority and marvel how far we have distanced ourselves from such foolishness. The fact is that idolatry is still very much alive and well. Many religions still worship idols, and their worshipers are emigrating from their homelands to settle among us. Also, when people live for their possessions—cars, houses, material goods, money—they are worshiping man-made things, not the Creator of the heavens and the earth. Such devotion is idolatry. In his discussion of the First Commandment in the Large Catechism, Martin Luther explained, "Now, I say that whatever you set your heart on and put your trust in is truly your god." In the time of need, the day of distress, and the hour of death, only the Lord God is our salvation.

2 Jonah's Deliverance *(2:10)*

Jonah's prayer of deliverance is bookended by two short verses—the first describing how "the Lord appointed a great fish to swallow up Jonah," and the other describing how "the Lord spoke to the fish, and it vomited Jonah out upon the dry land."

Jonah's three-day adventure in the belly of the fish, then, was God's doing. It began in terror and ended in deliverance. We can learn from this when we go through especially difficult experiences. God was there in the beginning; He is with us as we call upon Him; and He may at the proper time deliver us and give us relief.

We are not told where the fish "vomited" Jonah onto the dry land. Perhaps it was somewhere north of Israel, placing him closer to Nineveh, but it is likely that he came up on the shore of the Holy Land from where he had tried to flee, perhaps even at Joppa, the seaport from which he had departed.

3 Jonah Goes to Nineveh *(3:1 5)*

(V. 1) "The word of the Lord came to Jonah." But notice that this time the passage begins with "Then" instead of "Now," while adding, "the second time." God is starting over with Jonah by starting in the same way. Everything Jonah did before this didn't change a thing. God still wanted him at Nineveh; the job was the same. On the one hand, this may seem frustrating. On the other hand, we all love a do-over, a fresh chance for success. Seeing God do just that for Jonah should teach us something about our moments of failure, our place in God's grand plan. He still calls us. He still uses us for His purposes. The text goes on to repeat God's command, (v. 2) "Arise, go to Nineveh, that great city." God's commission remained the same. What changed was Jonah's response. This time, instead of reading (1:3) "But Jonah rose to flee," we read, (3:3) "So Jonah arose and went to Nineveh." He picked himself up off the beach, since now he had come to realize that one cannot undo God's plans.

As will soon become evident, however, Jonah remained an unwilling missionary (ch. 4)—if not in his actions, at least in his attitude. He carried out his mission, but not with hopes of accomplishing it. So Jonah proclaimed to the city, (3:4) "Yet forty days, and Nineveh shall be overthrown!" No doubt this is but a summary of his message. Yet even in this brief synopsis, we see both Law—"shall be overthrown"—and Gospel—"forty days." God was giving the city a time of grace, a time to turn.

As was the case with the sailors, Jonah's preaching bore surprising fruit: (v. 5) "And the people of Nineveh believed God." The Word of God is powerful in and of itself; it does not depend on the attitude or motivation of the people who proclaim it. Through the prophet Isaiah, God declares, (55:10–11)

> For as the rain and the snow come down from heaven
> and do not return there but water the earth,
> making it bring forth and sprout,
> giving seed to the sower and bread to the eater,
> so shall My word be that goes out from My mouth;
> it shall not return to Me empty,
> but it shall accomplish that which I purpose,
> and shall succeed in the thing for which I sent it.

Theologians use the term *efficacious*. That is, it works.

How reassuring it is to know that the effectiveness of the Word does not depend on the perfection of the messenger! The power of God's Word comes from the holy and omnipotent God and not from the person delivering the message. St. Paul put it this way: (1 Corinthians 2:3–5)

> And I was with you in weakness and in fear and much trembling, and my speech and my message were not in plausible words of wisdom, but in demonstration of the Spirit and of power, so that your faith might not rest in the wisdom of men but in the power of God.

Of course, we want to have a willing and ready heart when it comes to doing the Lord's work. And how do we get that? Through that very same Word! Jonah had seemed to forget that the word he preached to others—repentance—also applied to himself. Can that happen to us? Yes, it can. That's why we need to apply God's Word to ourselves as well as share it with others.

The text in Jonah 3 makes a point of the greatness of ancient Nineveh, (v. 3) "an exceedingly great city, three days journey in breadth." Its population has been estimated as perhaps half a million people. But the expression "exceedingly great" may well suggest more than size, as it can also be rendered "important to God." Nineveh was a great city both in size and in the eyes of God. Although filled with idolaters, Nineveh mattered to the Lord, for God is "not wishing that any should perish, but that all should reach repentance" (2 Peter 3:9). God desires to reach out to all with the message of salvation.

4 The People of Nineveh Repent *(3:6–10)*

As the king of Nineveh heard the word proclaimed by Jonah, the text relates five things he did: (1) he rose from his throne, (2) removed his robe, (3) covered himself with sackcloth, (4) sat in ashes, and (5) issued a proclamation. He didn't just sit where he was and brush the prophet's word aside; the king's actions showed *he* was repentant. After removing his royal robe, he put on sackcloth and sat in ashes. In ancient times, these actions were signs of sorrow. For example, when Job was afflicted, he tore his rob, shaved his head, and sat in ashes (Job 1–2).

For Nineveh's king, these were signs of sorrow and repentance. His proclamation to the people showed that the king understood the real meaning of repentance. Indeed, he told the people to fast—another sign of sorrow. But he spoke of more than the outward signs. He said, (Jonah 3:8–9) "Let them call out mightily to God. Let everyone turn from his evil way. . . . God may turn and relent and turn from His fierce anger." Earlier, the sailors had "called out to the Lord" (1:14). And centuries later, the apostle Paul would affirm that salvation is for all people: (Romans 10:12–13) "For there is no distinction between Jew and Greek; for the same Lord is Lord of all, bestowing His riches on all who call on Him. For 'everyone who calls on the name of the Lord will be saved.' "

The word "turn" contains a key concept in regard to repentance. An Old Testament Hebrew word for repent is *shuv*, which means "turn"; it is the word used here of Nineveh when the king told the people to turn from evil. Another word is *nachem* (used in Jonah 3:9–10; 4:2); it has the idea of being comforted (it is the root meaning of the prophet Nahum's name). The two words are used both of people and of God. When God repents (or relents), it is not a repentance from evil but an adjustment in His actions toward people. The people of Nineveh repented, and God relented from punishing them.

In the New Testament, the basic word for "repent" is *metanoia*, which involves a change of mind—a change of mind about what one has done or intended to do. It is a turning from our way of seeing ourselves to God's way. Jesus and the apostles preached repentance—that people change their minds and turn from their evil ways. Jesus said, (Matthew 4:17) "Repent, for the kingdom of heaven is at hand." Also, in the first of Martin Luther's Ninety-Five Theses, he wrote, "When our Lord and Master Jesus Christ said 'Repent,' He intended that the entire life of believers should be repentance." For Christians, then, our life is a constant struggle against our sinful nature, acknowledging that we daily sin much and rely on God's mercy and grace.

Repentance plays a large role in the Book of Jonah, and, as a matter of fact, in all of Scripture. Repentance consists of two aspects: sorrow over sin (contrition) and faith in God's forgiveness. It is the Law that brings about contrition, and the Gospel that brings about faith. Sometimes, Scripture includes both aspects under the one term *repentance*, and at other times the two aspects are distinct. For example, the opening chapter of Mark's Gospel says, (1:14–15) "Jesus came into Galilee, proclaiming the gospel of God, and saying, 'The time is fulfilled, and the kingdom of God is at hand; repent and believe in the gospel' "; in this case, the word "repent" would refer to the sorrow over sin, and the word "believe" would refer to faith in the Gospel. The king and people of Nineveh were sorry for their wicked ways, and they called out in faith to God for mercy. And God was merciful.

Even as Jonah 3 announces the story of Nineveh's repentance, it is also a chapter about God's patience and love—both with Nineveh and with Jonah. God was patient with Nineveh, and, in love, He gave the people of Nineveh time to repent—"yet forty days." God was also patient with Jonah and, in love, had given him a second opportunity to go to Nineveh and proclaim His message. God's patience and love extend to us today as well. As Scripture elsewhere says, (Numbers 14:18) "The Lord is slow to anger and abounding in steadfast love, forgiving iniquity and transgression."

Compelled by Christ's love, we will seek to exhibit that same attitude toward others. When we are tempted to be impatient and unloving toward others, we can think of this chapter. We can meditate about how the Lord has dealt with us in the past and how He continues to bless us.

5 Jonah and Christ's Resurrection—Miracles

The modern mind is not easily given to belief in miracles, and many today question or hold suspect most, if not all, of Scripture's miracles. In our scientific age, people want proof: "I'll believe it when I see it."

But Scripture tells us that Jonah did not remain in the belly of the great fish. Nor did Christ remain in the tomb. There is a comical element to Jonah's story that might make us reluctant to accept the historical nature of Jonah's miraculous deliverance, but is it easier to believe that Jesus came out of the tomb on the third day after He died?

A few words are in place at this point. We need to keep in mind that skepticism is not new with the modern world. When Mary miraculously became pregnant, Joseph's first thought was "to divorce her quietly" (Matthew 1:19), until in a dream an angel of the Lord assured him that this was from the Holy Spirit. At the other end of Jesus' life on earth, following His resurrection from the dead, when the disciples "saw Him they worshiped Him, but some doubted" (Matthew 28:17).

That being said, ours is an age that is much given to the response of "doubting" Thomas, who when told of Christ's resurrection, said, (John 20:25) "Unless I see in His hands the mark of the nails, and place my finger into the mark of the nails, and place my hand into His side, I will never believe." When Jesus a week later appeared to Thomas, the disciple fell to his knees and exclaimed to Jesus, (vv. 28–29) "My Lord and my God!" To which, the risen Savior responded, "Blessed are those who have not seen and yet have believed."

Many Christians are willing to say, "Well, I can accept the resurrection of Jesus. After all, He is divine. But the story of Jonah in the belly of the fish is stretching it a bit too far." The hitch is that Jesus used Jonah as a pattern—one real historical event foreshadowing the other. We can conclude, then, that Jonah's miraculous deliverance from within the great fish really happened, even as Jesus really rose from the dead.

Conclusion

Jonah's closing words of prayer from the belly of the fish proclaimed, (Jonah 2:9) "Salvation belongs to the Lord!" God delivered him miraculously and then went on to forgive the city of Nineveh. Which was more of a miracle? It reminds us of when Jesus healed a paralyzed man. Before performing the miracle, He told the man that his sins were forgiven. The scribes and Pharisees who were watching thought this was blasphemous, for only God can forgive sins. Jesus then said to them, (Luke 5:23) "Which is easier, to say, 'Your sins are forgiven you,' or to say, 'Rise and walk'?"

Jesus, who is both God and man, has power over the physical world; after all, He created it. He also has the power to forgive sins, for He came into the world to save it from sin and damnation. That, too, is a miracle. God has given us the gift of life and all its attendant blessings. Through His Word and the Sacraments of Baptism and the Lord's Supper, He gives us the gift of forgiveness and its accompanying blessings—salvation and eternal life in heaven.

Concluding Activities

Conclude the session with an appropriate prayer and distribute the study leaflet for week 4.

Should Not I Pity Nineveh?

Jonah 4

Preparing for the Session

Central Focus

Self-centeredness and prejudices against others are deeply ingrained in sinful human nature, even among those who serve the Lord, and yet God would have us know that His boundless love extends to all people.

Objectives

That participants, led by the Holy Spirit working through God's Word, will

1. see in Jonah's anger their own prejudices;
2. marvel at God's grace toward this fallen world; and
3. reach out to all with God's love in Christ.

Note for the small-group leaders: Lesson notes and other materials you will need begin on page 61.

For the Lecture Leader

Session Plan

Worship

Begin the session with the hymn printed in the study leaflet. Accompaniments are available in denominational hymnals, such as *Lutheran Service Book* or *Lutheran Worship* (refer to hymnal index). (Note: Concordia Publishing House has available *The Concordia Organist*. All the initial worship hymns in the LifeLight courses are included in this resource. It's especially helpful for mission congregations and small parishes. See the list of study resources on p. 7.) Follow with this prayer:

Prayer

O God, in pity, You reach out to this fallen world. You have graciously brought us to faith in Your Son, our Savior. Forgive us for the times when, rather than sharing this Gospel, we have kept it from others. Enable us to reflect Your love toward all people, through Jesus Christ, Your Son, our Lord, who lives and reigns with You and the Holy Spirit, one God, now and forever. Amen.

Lecture Presentation

Introduction

Bible commentators like to point out the sharp contrast between the end of Jonah chapter 3 and the beginning of chapter 4. The former ends on a note of ascendant joy—Nineveh has repented, and God's anger has relented. Perhaps the words from Jesus' parable of the lost sheep come to mind: (Luke 15:7) "Just so, I tell you, there will be more joy in heaven over one sinner who repents than over ninety-nine righteous persons who need no repentance."

There may have been joy in heaven over the repentance of Nineveh, but there was no joy in the heart of the prophet who had preached to those people. The final chapter of Jonah begins on a note of anger and despair.

1 Jonah's Anger *(4:1–3)*

Jonah had not been able to deter God's plan. After the unwilling missionary preached in Nineveh, the people repented. Now, instead of rejoicing in the conversion of this Gentile city, Jonah "was angry." The opening words of this chapter—"it displeased Jonah exceedingly"—literally say, "It was evil to Jonah, a great evil." To Jonah, it seemed unfair that this wicked city should enjoy God's forgiveness, His grace. And the words following—"was angry"—are literally, "and it inflamed him." Jonah saw the deliverance of Nineveh as a terrible evil, and so it inflamed him with anger.

Do we sometimes have an attitude like that of Jonah? Some people, we may feel, are simply undeserving of God's mercy. Discussing the possible conversion of a mass murderer before his death, this writer recalls an individual remarking, "If he's going to heaven, I don't want to be there." If we are honest with ourselves, we might admit there are certain people we don't think should be in heaven—they simply don't deserve it. The fact is, however, that in God's sight we are all undeserving. In the words of Isaiah, (64:6) "We have all become like one who is unclean, and all our righteous deeds are like a polluted garment" ["filthy rags" in the King James Version]. Or, as St. Paul put it, "all have sinned and fall short of the glory of God" (Romans 3:23).

Jonah knew that God is "a gracious God and merciful, slow to anger and abounding in steadfast love, and relenting from disaster." He knew it, for example, from God's words to Moses at Mount Sinai, when God declared concerning Himself: (Exodus 34:6–7) "The Lord, the Lord, a God merciful and gracious, slow to anger, and abounding in steadfast love and faithfulness, keeping steadfast love for thousands, forgiving iniquity and transgression and sin."

Discouraged and angered, Jonah pleaded with God, (4:3) "O Lord, please take my life from me." Like many other expressions in Jonah, this is similar to a comment from Elijah, who became discouraged when he seemed to be the only remaining believer; He prayed, "O Lord, take away my life" (1 Kings 19:4). Elijah had prayed those words because he thought everyone else had turned from the Lord in unbelief; Jonah prayed the same words because people had come to believe in the Lord! As he had done in the belly of the fish, Jonah prayed. The first time, he prayed to be delivered from death. Here he prayed to be delivered from life.

What was the reason for Jonah's state of mind? Actually, there were several factors that no doubt contributed to it. Nineveh was well-known as a wicked city; the savagery of the Assyrian armies was legendary. More than that, though, Nineveh was an enemy of Judah, which was the place where God's holy temple stood and where God's chosen people dwelled. The prophets Hosea (10:6) and Isaiah (7:17, 20) foretold that someday Assyria would overrun Israel and—in Hosea's prophecy—take it into captivity. These prophets might have carried out their work toward the tail end of Jonah's ministry, so he may have been aware of such predictions. Whether he was or not, he knew Assyria was an idolatrous nation, and he knew that the children of Israel were God's chosen people.

How could God even think of being gracious to them? Jonah was angry—perhaps at the people of Nineveh for their repentance, perhaps somewhat at himself for his preaching, but mostly at God for His steadfast love.

2 The Lord's Question *(4:4)*

Instead of firing back at His angry and prejudiced prophet, God simply asked a question: "Do you do well to be angry?" Some translations transmit the idea in a slightly different (and less literal) way: Do you have any right to be angry?

There is a time for righteous anger—against injustice, against persistent hardness of heart. This was not such a time. Scripture tells us, (Psalm 103:8) "The Lord is merciful and gracious, slow to anger and abounding in steadfast love," and it goes on to say that we should strive to be the same: (James 1:19) "Let every person be quick to hear, slow to speak, slow to anger." Jonah has demonstrated the all-too-human tendency to be quick to anger.

The Lord tells us, (Proverbs 15:1) "A soft answer turns away wrath, but a harsh word stirs up anger." Here, He came to Jonah with a gentle question. When Elijah was near despair, the Lord had also spoken to him—not in the strong wind, the earthquake, or the fire He sent, but in a gentle or low "whisper" (1 Kings 19:11–13). God speaks to us in the quiet of His Word. His message need not be blared from a pulpit, a lectern, or a loudspeaker, but it can come in quiet or in silent reading at the bedside.

We can apply God's question to ourselves when we're upset. "Do you do well to be angry?" Is it because God is not doing things the way we think He should? Is it because others who seem less deserving are getting as much or more than we are? Jonah had no reply.

3 God Preserves Jonah *(4:5–6)*

Jonah had no reply to God's question. Instead, he went out of the city; made a "booth," a temporary shelter; and sat down to see "what would become of the city." What did he wait to see? Apparently, he was hoping that Nineveh's repentance had been insincere and that it would suffer the same fate as Sodom and Gomorrah (Genesis 19:24), upon which unrepentant cities God rained fire and sulfur (or as the better known wording of the King James Version has it, fire and brimstone). Or maybe Jonah was hoping that the repentance of the Ninevites would be very short-lived and that they would quickly return to their wicked ways and reap the rewards thereof.

But that didn't happen. God was merciful to the repentant city of Nineveh. He also was merciful to the prejudiced prophet. (4:6) "God appointed a plant and made it come up over Jonah, that it might be a shade over his head, to save him from his discomfort." After all, this was a desert land, where people desperately needed shade. The region of ancient Assyria, modern-day Iraq, has long, hot, dry summers, broken only by short and cool (not cold) winters. Apparently, then, this journey to Nineveh took place in the sweltering summer. We can picture the scene: while Jonah, contrary to God's will, impatiently watches for signs of Nineveh's destruction, God is patient with Jonah and protects him.

Commentators are not sure of the identification of the plant: some have suggested it was a castor oil plant; others a gourd, a vine, a leafy plant, or simply a plant. As was the case with the great fish that swallowed Jonah, the exact species of this plant that God caused to grow so quickly is not important; the lesson is important.

Seemingly unappreciative of the irony of his situation, Jonah was "exceedingly glad because of the plant." We cannot but wonder how many times God lovingly puts up with us, as He did with Jonah, always arranging things for our good, while we fail to see ourselves as we really are. We wonder why God doesn't strike down the evil people of the world, while we might rather be asking why God is not striking us down. It is because He is gracious—not only to others, but to us as well.

4 Jonah's Complaint *(4:7–8)*

Jonah was glad for the shelter, but he still had a lesson to learn. Even though God had preserved him miraculously for a second time, the prophet still had an attitude of bitterness toward Nineveh—and ultimately toward the Lord for preserving the city. Now the Lord began toying with Jonah, and the next day He removed the sheltering plant. Just as He had "appointed a plant" (and earlier, had "appointed a great fish to swallow up Jonah"), He now "appointed a worm" to destroy the plant; on top of that, God "appointed a scorching east wind." As always, God was in control. He is the creator and Lord of nature, and in these cases He used nature in miraculous ways.

The Bible teaches us that in His wisdom God gives and God removes. When Job lost his many possessions as well as all his children, he declared, (Job 1:21) "Naked I came from my mother's womb, and naked shall I return. The Lord gave, and the Lord has taken away; blessed be the name of the Lord." Although Job later faltered and argued that God was being unfair, he remained constant in his commitment to God as the source of goodness, life, and even the resurrection from the dead (Job 19). Jonah had yet to arrive at such constancy.

Commentators have pointed out that up to this point in the story of Jonah, the covenant name, the Lord (Yahweh or Jehovah), has been used (for God's own explanation of that name, see Exodus 34:6–7). Now, as He removed from Jonah the protective plant, the generic title "God" appears. This was how Jonah had wanted God to treat Nineveh, not as the gracious Lord, but as the condemning God. We should not get the impression that the designations *Lord* and *God* always carry either a Law or Gospel connection. Yet it is striking that at this turn in the story, God withdraws the covenant name. In the withering of the vine, Jonah received a close-up look at God's destructive powers, and he did not like it.

The Lord had given the plant for Job, and now He removed it. Sadly, Jonah's response was once again a request to die: (4:8) "It is better for me to die than to live." Although we might fault Jonah here, this is not necessarily an expression of unbelief. Believers do at times wish to be with the Lord, as Paul wrote to the Philippian Christians, (Philippians 1:21–24)

> For to me to live is Christ, and to die is gain. If I am to live in the flesh, that means fruitful labor for me. Yet which I shall choose I cannot tell. I am hard pressed between the two. My desire is to depart and be with Christ, for that is far better. But to remain in the flesh is more necessary on your account.

In contrast to that, Jonah's wish came from bitterness; he did not want to see Nineveh enjoy God's mercy.

5 God's Love *(4:9–11)*

God was not done with Jonah. Again the question came, "Do you do well to be angry"—this time adding "for the plant?" Jonah was concerned about the plant, even though he had neither created it nor made it grow. At this juncture, the text returns to the covenant name: "And the Lord said, . . ." The final words of the book consist of this short message from the Lord.

The Almighty had provided the plant. Having pointed that out to Jonah, God asked a rhetorical question: "And should not I pity Nineveh, that great city?" The Lord proceeds to point out the inhabitants of the city: 120,000 people, "who do not know their right hand from their left," and many cattle.

The phrase about not knowing their right hand from their left alludes to people who have no discernment. It could refer to all the people of the city—people living in spiritual ignorance—or to the children of the city—that is, the young and naïve. Since we do not know the population of the city, either interpretation could work. A city of 120,000 may have been large in the ancient world; a city with 120,000 children and perhaps a total population of around half a million would certainly have been "great." Whatever the size, God cared for each and every inhabitant. Not only that, He also cared for all the animals, for even though they do not have human souls, they, too, are part of His creation.

How unfathomable is God's love! His concern extends to all creation. Jesus reminds us, (Matthew 10:29–31)

> Are not two sparrows sold for a penny? And not one of them will fall to the ground apart from your Father. But even the hairs of your head are all numbered. Fear not, therefore; you are of more value than many sparrows.

Whether Jonah had a change of heart, the text does not say. The existence of the Book of Jonah would suggest that in humility and repentance, Jonah recorded these events from his life. He ends not with his own final words on the subject, but with God's. From ancient times, the book was read on the Day of Atonement, as a reminder of God's mercy and forgiveness. It continues to point to God's love for all people of every language and place and time.

Conclusion

The Book of Jonah differs from the other prophets in that few of his actual words are recorded. His words to the sailor and to Nineveh are very brief summaries of what he actually said. Rather than being a book that records Jonah's preaching, the book records his personal story, his interaction with the Lord. Although the other prophets (in particular, a good share of Daniel) contain some biographical information (in the case of Obadiah and Micah, very little), the books are basically the words they spoke and recorded as they were inspired by the Holy Spirit. For that reason, it is easier to see ourselves in the person of Jonah. We see someone who takes up God's calling, but reluctantly. We see someone who too readily wishes good for himself and disaster for those who are different from him. And in God's patient dealing with this very down-to-earth figure, we are reminded how patient our Savior is with us and how slow we so often are to listen.

In reading the last chapter of Jonah, we might marvel as this prophet's sheer obstinacy. He wanted things to go his way—my way or the highway. Yet is not Jonah in many ways a mirror being held up to our own sinful tendencies? How stubbornly we cling to our prejudices! How slowly we let go our notions of how God is supposed to do things in our life and in the lives of others!

God is at work in our lives, though we, like Jonah beneath the leafy plant, don't always see it. Often without acknowledging God's role, we are glad when life is pleasant, and we are upset with others and with God when disappointment comes our way. Yet He has given us more than we ask and in ways beyond our comprehension. He has given us the gift of life and all the other blessings that we have enjoyed along our earthly pilgrimage.

Above all, He has given us His Son, in whom and through whom we enjoy forgiveness, salvation, and an endless future in heaven. As St. Paul wrote to the Ephesian Church (3:20–21), "Now to Him who is able to do far more abundantly than all that we ask or think, according to the power at work within us, to Him be glory in the church and in Christ Jesus throughout all generations, forever and ever. Amen"

Concluding Activities

Conclude the session with an appropriate prayer and distribute the study leaflet for week 5.

The Lord Is Coming

Micah 1

Preparing for the Session

Central Focus

There is nothing new under the sun. People today, as in ancient times, still need the message of God's Law to show them their sin and the Gospel to show them their salvation.

Objectives

That participants, led by the Holy Spirit working through God's Word, will

1. pay attention to Scripture's warnings;
2. compare the idolatry of Micah's time with that of today; and
3. distinguish ever more clearly between Law and Gospel.

Note for the small-group leaders: Lesson notes and other materials you will need begin on page 63.

For the Lecture Leader

Session Plan

Worship

Begin the session with the hymn printed in the study leaflet. Accompaniments are available in denominational hymnals, such as *Lutheran Service Book* or *Lutheran Worship* (refer to hymnal index). (Note: Concordia Publishing House has available *The Concordia Organist.* All the initial worship hymns in the LifeLight courses are included in this resource. It's especially helpful for mission congregations and small parishes. See the list of study resources on p. 7.) Follow with this prayer:

Prayer

O Lord, beneath whom the mountains melt and the valleys are split, how awesome is Your power, how terrible Your judgments! Because of our sins, we deserve nothing but punishment both now and forever. Forgive us, and strengthen our faith, as we cling to Your promises of mercy, through Jesus Christ, Your Son, our Lord, who lives and reigns with You and the Holy Spirit, one God, now and forever. Amen.

Lecture Presentation

Introduction

Following the first three kings of Israel—Saul, David, and Solomon—the kingdom split into two parts. The northern part, with its capital in Samaria, was known as Israel, and the southern part, with its capital in Jerusalem, was known as Judah. For a period of about two centuries, this situation continued, until 722 BC, when Israel fell to the Assyrian armies. After this, the Northern Kingdom ceased to exist as a nation. A little more than a century later, the Southern Kingdom was overrun by the Babylonians. By God's grace, the Judeans continued as a distinct people; this was necessary, for God promised that the Savior of the world would come from the line of Judah and from this land. As we shall see, Micah would prophesy that this Savior would come from the small town of Bethlehem, only about five miles south of Jerusalem.

1 Micah and Isaiah

Micah was a contemporary of Isaiah, the most famous of the Old Testament prophets. They lived about seven centuries before the coming of Christ. If Christians know anything about the Book of Micah, almost certainly it is the prophecy of Bethlehem as the birthplace of the Savior (5:2), referred to in the Gospel of Matthew (2:6). Beyond that, sadly, many would have to shrug their shoulders in ignorance about Micah's book. Nevertheless, among the Minor Prophets, the Book of Micah is fairly substantial in length (seven chapters, making it longer than all but three of the Minor Prophets) and is replete with thunderous proclamations of God's judgment along with sweet messages of God's love and forgiveness.

Like Isaiah, Micah foretold the destruction of the nation of Judah and the great city of Jerusalem. The prophecy that Jerusalem would "become a heap of ruins" (3:12) would be fulfilled when the Babylonians, under King Nebuchadnezzar, destroyed the city, along with the glorious temple of Solomon, and took the people into captivity in distant Babylon.

Throughout the Bible run the threads of Law and Gospel. The Law is the aspect of Scripture that speaks of God's commands, along with His warnings of judgment, punishment, death, and damnation. The Law strikes fear into the arrogant, and, like a mirror, it shows us all our blemishes and faults. The Gospel, on the other hand, contains God's promises, along with His pronouncements of mercy, grace, forgiveness, life, and salvation. The Gospel brings relief to consciences laden with guilt as it freely offers eternal life in heaven through Jesus, the Christ.

To distinguish properly between the Law and the Gospel is the highest art—easy in theory, yet challenging in real-life practice. This distinction is the key to understanding the Old Testament prophets. Their writings pronounce the Law in all its fury, and they set forth the Gospel in all its glory. The Book of Micah is replete with both. Micah moves from prophecies of doom to prophecies of sweet comfort, from warnings of God's wrath upon evil to promises of divine deliverance and restoration.

2 Warning *(1:1–4)*

As is the case with other prophets, Micah opens his book by asserting that the words he is recording are not his, but "the word of the Lord." It came to Micah at a specific time in history, during the reigns of Jotham, Ahaz, and Hezekiah, kings of Judah from 750 to 686 BC. Micah does not say how God's Word came to him—whether in a dream, a vision, or some other means. Whenever and however God spoke to the prophets and through them, the revelation was always in keeping with previous Scripture, beginning with the Books of Moses—that is, the first five books of the Bible, also known as the Pentateuch. Moreover, the words of God's inspired prophets always proved to be true, whether speaking of contemporary issues or of things to come.

The three kings during whose reigns Micah carried out his prophetic work were, of course, descendants of David and Solomon. Little is known about Jotham, who was faithful to God (2 Kings 15:34). His son Ahaz was wicked: (2 Kings 16:2) "he did not do what was right in the eyes of the Lord his God, as his father [forefather] David had done." Disgusted with his father Ahaz's wickedness, Hezekiah served the Lord; although he faltered later in life, he humbled himself and repented, and has gone down in history as one of Judah's more illustrious kings (see 2 Kings 18:1–6; 2 Chronicles 32:25–26). It was during the twenty-nine year reign of Hezekiah that the Assyrian armies swept down upon Jerusalem and besieged the city. Micah, then, lived during a dangerous and tumultuous time, when forces of evil were struggling mightily against God, both among leaders and among the people at large. It was a time not so much unlike our own.

During the reigns of these kings, the people of Judah were constantly living on edge, especially because of the threat of the mighty Assyrian empire to the north. In Micah's lifetime, the Northern Kingdom of Israel fell to Assyria, and the Southern Kingdom was forced into paying tribute to the Assyrians. Refugees came from the north as well as from territory that was ceded to Philistia. Given these circumstances, the Judeans ended up bearing a heavy tax burden, the economic gap between rich and poor widened, and Micah had to excoriate the wealthy people of Judah who were taking advantage of their own impoverished countrymen (Micah 2:1–4).

Micah identifies himself as from Moresheth, a relatively small town of Judah located perhaps twenty miles southwest of Jerusalem and near the border of Philistia, the perennial enemy of God's people. Aside from his hometown and the dating of his prophecy, little else is known about this prophet. His name means "Who is like the Lord?" (Hebrew: *Micahyahu*). This faithful small-town prophet boldly proclaimed God's message to Jerusalem, the legendary city of kings, and to countless people down through the ages. As he says, "Pay attention, O earth, and all that is in it." His message is for people of every time and place.

The Book of Micah's prophecy begins with the word "Hear," as God calls the people to pay attention to what He has to say. This call to hear is repeated in 3:1 and 6:1.

3 Judgment against Samaria and Jerusalem *(1:5–7)*

Although directed to people everywhere, Micah's prophecy focuses on Samaria and Jerusalem. Samaria, the capital of the Northern Kingdom, was destroyed in 721 BC, during the time of Micah's ministry. God, through Micah, declared this would happen: (1:6) "I will make Samaria a heap in the open country."

That generation would witness the fall and deportation of the tribes of Israel—a disaster from which the

Northern Kingdom would never recover. Throughout the centuries, people have speculated as to what became of the "lost ten tribes" of Israel—with theories connecting them to peoples as divergent as the English and Native Americans. The reality is that while some stayed behind on the land, many were taken into exile and absorbed by the Assyrians, as the intertestamental Book of Tobit describes.

The capital of the Southern Kingdom, Jerusalem, would fall to the Babylonians more than a century later, but early in this section, Micah zeroes in on Samaria: (v. 7) "and all her idols I will lay waste." Surrounded by idolatrous nations—whose worship of man-made gods included temple prostitution and child sacrifice—the people of Israel and Judah had succumbed to the temptation to take part in such worship. In so doing, they would bring God's judgment upon themselves and upon the physical city of Samaria: (v. 6) "I will pour down her stones into the valley and uncover her foundations."

The Assyrians would destroy the idols of Samaria, says Micah, only to replace them with their own idols. And even as temple prostitution was connected with ancient idolatry, God says that the earnings from this practice would also be lost. The treasures of Samaria would be taken by the Assyrians, who in turn would use them in the service of their own temples, in the worship of their own gods.

To help set the chronology of Assyria and its capital Nineveh in order, we can look at key events relating to the Assyrian interchange with Bible history:

931 BC—Following the death of King Solomon, the kingdom of Israel splits into two rival nations: Israel (Northern Kingdom) and Judah (Southern Kingdom)

c. 900—Assyria arises as a superpower

c. 875—Nineveh develops as a great city of Assyria

790—Jonah preaches in Nineveh; the city repents

c. 750 to 680—Micah and Isaiah preach in Judah

722—Northern Kingdom of Israel with capital of Samaria conquered by Assyria

c. 700—Assyrians overrun much of Judah, stopped at Jerusalem

c. 650—The prophet Nahum foretells the fall of Nineveh

612—Nineveh falls to the Babylonians

During the lifetime of Micah, the Assyrians were on the march, even as Micah prophesied. They came with their two- or four-horse chariots; with their cavalry in units of perhaps a thousand; with archers, each of whom had up to fifty arrows in their quivers; with slingers, who carried stones; with lancers and their iron-tipped lances; and with infantrymen carrying shields, wearing armor and crested helmets, and carrying a sword, or maybe two.

The assault on Samaria began in 725 BC and ended three years later under the Assyrian King Sargon II, who boasted about how he besieged and broke the city to lead away tens of thousands of captives in fear and trembling.

The Lord, the King of kings, gave the real reason behind the fall of the city and the Northern Kingdom: (Micah 1:5) "All this is for the transgression of Jacob and for the sins of the house of Israel."

4 Lament *(1:8–9)*

Now the prophet speaks for himself: (v. 8) "I will lament and wail." The idolatrous practices that had come from the pagan nations and infected Samaria would spread south, like a plague or like the Black Death, and would poison Judah: (v. 9) "For her wound is incurable, and it has come to Judah; it has reached the gate of My people, to Jerusalem."

We cannot but think of our own times, how the cancers of humanism, rationalism, and materialism are eating away at and destroying our societies and even civilizations. God has been replaced by man at the center of life (humanism). Our human reason arrogantly asserts itself above the Holy Scriptures and mocks God's Word (rationalism). The things of this world—houses, entertainment, shiny new vehicles—call out, not unlike the captivating idols in ancient temples, to the hearts and minds and very souls of men and women: "Devote yourselves to a life of money and all it can buy" (materialism).

Just as the idolatry had spread into Judah, so would the wages of sin spread. Assyrians would soon ransack the country's towns. They would be stopped short of the ultimate prize and be turned back at Jerusalem only during the reign of King Hezekiah. But later, after a period of respite, the city would indeed fall to the Babylonians.

5 The Enemies Advance *(1:10–16)*

While the people concern themselves with their idols, enemy armies are on the march, like the lions depicted in stone in their palaces, drawing ever closer to their prey. In a somber dirge, Micah mentions towns that are representative of Judah.

The various names also serve as plays on words, relating to the sound or to the meaning of the names, as the prophet includes a comment along with the designation of each town. Gath (a Philistine city whose name sounds like the Hebrew word for "tell"): "Tell it not" (lest they, like the Edomites of Obadiah, gloat over Judah's fall [see also 2 Samuel 1:20]). Beth-le-aphrah ("house of dust"): "roll yourselves in the dust." Shaphir ("beautiful"): "pass on your way . . . in nakedness and shame." Zaanan (sounds like "come out"): "do not come out." Beth-ezel ("house at the side of"): "shall take away from you its standing place." This last town is mentioned only here in all of Scripture.

For the remainder of the list, we simply list the towns and their meanings: Maroth (sounds like "bitter"); Lachish (a larger, fortified city; sounds like "team"); Moresheth-gath (Micah's hometown; sounds like the word for "dowry"—here attached with the word Gath, probably because it was close to that Philistine city); Achzib (means "deception"); Mareshah (means "conqueror"); Adullam ("retreat"—God Himself would come here in judgment).

The term "daughter of Zion" is a common biblical term for the inhabitants of Jerusalem. It is familiar from the Palm Sunday story of Jesus' triumphal entrance into Jerusalem. Quoting from the prophet Zechariah, the evangelist writes: (Matthew 21:4–5; cf. Zechariah 9:9)

> This took place to fulfill what was spoken by the prophet, saying,
>
> "Say to the daughter of Zion,
> 'Behold, your king is coming to you,
> humble, and mounted on a donkey,
> on a colt, the foal of a beast of burden.'"

This dirge of names would be something akin to our saying of two of today's most famous cities, "New York, go find yourself new work," or, "Los Angeles, have you lost your guardian angels?" Micah, however, was using the names of regular towns in this way, not the major city of Judah, Jerusalem. Incidentally, the name Jerusalem means "city of peace," a name that would certainly lend itself to numerous plays on words. Yet, while the term "play on words" may fittingly describe Micah's references to the various towns, his usage was anything but playful. His words were stark warnings of judgment to come.

Sennacherib, king of Assyria, boasted that he took forty-six cities and plundered towns, carrying off more than 200,000 people and their livestock. He bragged that he did all this while Hezekiah hid himself in Jerusalem. Sennacherib failed to mention that his armies were turned back at Jerusalem.

In the closing verse of this chapter, God calls upon the people to shave their heads: (v. 16) "Make yourselves bald and cut off your hair." This was a sign of grief. The people of Judah would soon see the Assyrian invasion that would sweep away the Northern Kingdom of Israel and threaten the Southern Kingdom of Judah. They would not live to see the day when this prophecy would strike at the heart of Judah, as the armies of Babylon would take the people of that land into exile.

Conclusion

Although the towns mentioned in this section of Micah mean little to modern readers, they were very real places (many of them have been identified with present-day towns) inhabited by real people. Without much difficulty, we can put ourselves in their shoes, or more accurately, sandals. With the Assyrian armies headed toward Israel and Judah, many had to wonder when they might see a cloud of dust on the horizon—the Assyrian army. Yet as we can see from Micah, many people were unconcerned with that threat. They had given themselves over to the godless lifestyle of the times, caught up in the worship of gods that would prove useless in the day of disaster.

Years before the time of Micah, the once glorious kingdom of David and Solomon had been divided into the two adversarial nations of Israel and Judah. Now, in Micah's lifetime, Israel would fall, never to rise again, and Judah would be threatened with destruction. History never stands still. Nations rise only to become haughty and fall. In our lifetime, we have witnessed momentous challenges to the Western world. As in Micah's time, those challenges come both from within and from without. In the last century, two world wars shook civilization to its roots. Even more disturbing are the challenges from within, as Christian churches struggle against the forces of godlessness.

There is another similarity. God is still faithful and still watches over us. His promises remain unchanging—they are promises of forgiveness, life, and salvation in Jesus.

Concluding Activities

Conclude the session with an appropriate prayer and distribute the study leaflet for week 6.

Gather the Remnant

Micah 2–3

Preparing for the Session

Central Focus

Where is one to put his or her trust? To place one's trust in other human beings is foolish; God alone delivers when it comes to life on earth and in the world to come.

Objectives

That participants, led by the Holy Spirit working through God's Word, will

1. look to the almighty God, not earthly leaders, for assurance;
2. avoid false teachers who lead people astray; and
3. humble themselves before the Lord.

Note for the small-group leaders: Lesson notes and other materials you will need begin on page 65.

For the Lecture Leader

Session Plan

Worship

Begin the session with the hymn printed in the study leaflet. Accompaniments are available in denominational hymnals, such as *Lutheran Service Book* or *Lutheran Worship* (refer to hymnal index). (Note: Concordia Publishing House has available *The Concordia Organist.* All the initial worship hymns in the LifeLight courses are included in this resource. It's especially helpful for mission congregations and small parishes. See the list of study resources on p. 7.) Follow with this prayer:

Prayer

Almighty Father, how the world's high and mighty despise the preaching of Your Word and those who bring it! Yet You protect and gather the remnant of Your people. In these increasingly godless times, keep us in Your Word, and use us to share Your grace with a dying world, through Jesus, Your Son, our Lord, who lives and reigns with You and the Holy Spirit, one God, now and forever. Amen.

Lecture Presentation

Introduction

In the first chapter of Micah, the prophet denounced the idolatry of the people of Israel and Judah. In the second and third chapters, he turns to their leaders—the directors of businesses, the heads of state, and the religious authorities.

1 Woe to the Oppressors *(2:1–11)*

When people turn from God, they turn against one another. The worship of idols led to the hardening of people's hearts against one another. Micah speaks to those who lie awake at night thinking how they might take advantage of others and who then get up early and do it: (v. 1) "Woe to those who devise wickedness and work evil on their beds! When the morning dawns, they perform it."

The pronouncement of "woe" upon these wicked people reminds us how Jesus confronted the evil religious leaders of His day: (Matthew 23) "Woe to you, scribes and Pharisees . . ." Seven times, Jesus would use that word "woe" in the same discourse, as He went on to refer to them with the unflattering nomenclature of blind guides, whitewashed tombs, hypocrites, and serpents. As Micah pronounced God's judgment on Jerusalem 750 years earlier, Jesus declared to the city, (Matthew 23:37–38)

> O Jerusalem, Jerusalem, the city that kills the prophets and stones those who are sent to it! How often would I have gathered your children together as a hen gathers her brood under her wings, and you were not willing! See, your house is left to you desolate.

The prophets of the Old Testament were the preachers of the day. As Micah—and Jesus—clearly demonstrated, true prophets did not pull any punches when it came to speaking out against sin. Today there seems to be a widely held notion that preachers should say only what is politically correct, not come down too hard with the Law, and so on. The fear is that they might turn people away or that they might personally suffer repercussions from the high and mighty. Both might happen, and as

Jesus stated, the prophets of old were killed and stoned. We do not know the end of Micah, but according to tradition, his contemporary Isaiah "was sawed in two," as perhaps alluded to in the Book of Hebrews (11:35–38). Jesus, the quintessential Prophet, preached His way to the cross.

Sin must be spoken against. A true preaching of the Law is a statement of love, for it warns of the consequences of unrepented sin. How can anyone take the Gospel seriously if evil is not treated seriously? What is there to repent of and what is there to be saved from, if sin is treated lightly and the wages of sin are never mentioned?

So Micah goes into details about the sinful practices of his day (which can be easily applied to our day as well!). He talks about coveting and then taking fields, houses, and inheritances. Stealing begins in the heart with coveting—wanting something that is not ours to have. Three of the Ten Commandments deal with stealing (Seventh) and coveting (Ninth and Tenth): (Exodus 20:15, 17)

> You shall not steal. . . .
> You shall not covet your neighbor's house; you shall not covet your neighbor's wife, or his male servant, or his female servant, or his ox, or his donkey, or anything that is your neighbor's.

Because of such greediness, disaster would come "from which you cannot remove your necks." Although some translators see this expression as a reference about the people not being able to save themselves, this seems to be a reference to their future servitude under the Babylonians. For Jeremiah spoke, (28:14)

> Thus says the Lord of hosts, the God of Israel: "I have put upon the neck of all these nations an iron yoke to serve Nebuchadnezzar king of Babylon, and they shall serve him, for I have given to him even the beasts of the field."

From evil business practices, the text turns to wickedness among the spiritual leaders. Micah lets us in on the kind of response his preaching was met with: (2:6) " 'Do not preach'—thus they preach—'one should not preach of such things; disgrace will not overtake us.' " This was the same type of response Jeremiah would hear from Jerusalem a century and a half later. The true prophets were accused of being too negative. And talk of disaster was not what Micah's—or Jeremiah's—opponents wanted to hear. The false preachers, on the other hand, were telling their audiences what they wanted to hear.

In the New Testament, Paul put it this way in his final letter: (2 Timothy 4:3–4)

> For the time is coming when people will not endure sound teaching, but having itching ears they will accumulate for themselves teachers to suit their own passions, and will turn away from listening to the truth and wander off into myths.

Jesus warns us to beware of false prophets, and speaking through Jeremiah, God declares, (23:16–17)

> Thus says the Lord of hosts: "Do not listen to the words of the prophets who prophesy to you, filling you with vain hopes. They speak visions of their own minds, not from the mouth of the Lord. They say continually to those who despise the word of the Lord, 'It shall be well with you'; and to everyone who stubbornly follows his own heart, they say, 'No disaster shall come upon you.' "

Nor is it any different today. People do not like to hear sin denounced; they do not want to hear about God's judgment coming on an increasingly godless society. From pulpits across the land, people hear that everything is fine. To refer to an expression from the 1970s, "I'm okay; you're okay." The fact is that none of us is okay. We need to confess our sins and look to God's mercy and grace.

Meanwhile, society goes on with business as usual, but God has to say of His people, "My people have risen up as an enemy." Without thinking twice, the wicked take from the rich, drive out women from their houses, and take from children "My splendor forever." By not teaching the children God's truth, those responsible for training the next generation have deprived them of the blessings that only God can give. What a terrible legacy to pass on—a legacy of destruction!

Micah closes this section with some sarcasm. Someone who preaches wine and strong drink, "he would be the preacher for this people!" Yes, tell them what they want to hear, the good times will just keep rolling alone. Sadly, that's nothing but "wind and lies."

2 Mercy for the Remnant *(2:12–13)*

In the middle of such denunciations (with more to follow), we find a lovely passage of relief, appearing like an oasis in the desert of sin and desolation. Here, God speaks of His protection and care for "Jacob . . . the remnant of Israel." Jacob and Israel were two names for the father of the nation (see, for instance, comments on Obadiah 10–14 in Session 1). These names, especially the name Israel, came to signify the entire nation, the people who descended from him. In speaking of His concern for Israel, the Lord uses two images: that of a shepherd and that of a king.

The image of God as Shepherd is woven throughout the Bible, with the best-known passages being the beautiful psalm of David, (Psalm 23) "The Lord is my shepherd; I shall not want," and the words of Jesus, (John 10:11) "I am the good shepherd. The good shepherd lays down his life for the sheep." Here in Micah, God speaks of gathering the people "like a flock in its pasture." God looks ahead to the time when He will lead the people back from their captivity in Babylon to their homeland.

The closing verse shifts the imagery from that of a shepherd gathering the sheep to a picture of a king leading the people. The imagery of God as king is also common in both the Old and New Testaments. Following the Babylonian exile, the line of the kings of Judah was cut off; so the king who "passes on before them" is not an earthly king. Rather, it refers to God Himself. Through opened gates, the remnant will march out on their way back from captivity with "the Lord at their head."

Both images are beautiful illustrations of God's love and power. We know Jesus as our Lord and as our Good Shepherd (John 10). Although we like sheep have gone astray, He has laid down His life for us, and He leads us to quiet waters and green pastures. He is also our King (John 18:36). His kingdom is everlasting, and we will enjoy its full splendor in heaven.

3 Rulers and Prophets Corrupt *(3:1–4)*

Following the wonderful promise of deliverance, the text returns to the spiritual condition of Micah's day. The "heads of Jacob" and "rulers of the house of Israel" (a poetic manner of referring to the leaders of the people with two parallel descriptors) are the ones who should "know justice."

Instead, they have turned justice upside down: "you who hate the good and love the evil." Or to use the prophet Isaiah's expression, they "call evil good and good evil" (5:20). The leaders were figuratively consuming the people "like meat in a pot." Taking advantage of the helpless, the leaders exploited them; they ate them up and then spit them out. Not until it is too late, says Micah, will they try to turn to God, "but He will not answer them; He will hide His face from them."

Jesus says that on the Last Day, it will be like that: (Luke 13:25–28)

> When once the master of the house has risen and shut the door, and you begin to stand outside and to knock at the door, saying, "Lord, open to us," then He will answer you, "I do not know where you come from." Then you will begin to say, "We ate and drank in Your presence, and You taught in our streets." But He will say, "I tell you, I do not know where you come from. Depart from Me, all you workers of evil!" In that place there will be weeping and gnashing of teeth, when you see Abraham and Isaac and Jacob and all the prophets in the kingdom of God but you yourselves cast out.

Now is the day of salvation. To continue in wickedness and think that one can fool God with a token repentance at the last minute is worse than foolhardy. It is playing with the very fires of hell.

4 Rulers and Prophets Denounced *(3:5–12)*

Now the Lord directly points to the false prophets. They cry "peace" (see also Jeremiah 23). They say things are just fine, in particular to those who were paying them, "when they have something to eat." In other words, the false prophets changed their message according to what they were getting or not getting from people.

As a result of their living the lie, these "prophets" would no longer be able to distinguish truth from error any more. Instead of showing others the light, they themselves came to walk in darkness: "Therefore it shall be night to you, without vision, and darkness to you." It is tragic when leaders in churches lose their own way by placing human wisdom above God's revelation or by replacing God's treasure with the treasures of the world, material success and power (today's so-called gospel of success). An old term for prophet is "seer," one who sees. Ironically, the seers have become blind.

It is an irony that appears elsewhere in Scripture. On one occasion, after Jesus had given physical sight to a man who had been born blind, He said, (John 9:39) "For judgment I came into this world, that those who do not see may see, and those who see may become blind." The religious leaders of Jesus' day, like those of Micah's, because of their unbelief would not—could not—see the truth. Yet others who had been spiritually blind did come to believe God's Word and see. In the hymn "Amazing Grace," John Newton (1725–1807) captured the wonder of coming to faith and being able to see:

Amazing grace!—how sweet the sound—
That saved a wretch like me!
I once was lost, but now am found,
Was blind but now I see!

To return to Micah, not only do the seers become blind, but they, along with the diviners (those claiming they could predict the future) are also "put to shame." Ashamed, they cover their faces (here, "their lips"), for God does not answer their prayers.

Micah, on the other hand, is "filled with power, with the Spirit of the Lord." Guided by the Holy Spirit, he speaks God's truth, "to declare to Jacob his transgression and to Israel his sin." The final verses of the chapter hit hard at the rulers. They pervert justice and make what is straight "crooked"; they build the city, but with "blood" and "iniquity" on their hands; the leaders "give judgment for a bribe"; the "priests teach for a price"; the prophets make predictions "for money." Everything was turned upside down. Everything was turned inside out.

While all this was going on, these leaders brazenly asserted, "Is not the Lord in the midst of us? No disaster shall come upon us." They could not have been more wrong. To make matters even more disastrous, the coming ruin would be on their heads. "Therefore because of you . . . Jerusalem shall become a heap of ruins." They had the awesome responsibility of serving God's people, but instead they served only themselves.

Again, we marvel at how closely the times of the prophets are mirrored in our own day. In lands once so richly blessed with the faithful preaching of the Gospel, the light grows dimmer as so many would-be shepherds and their sheep grope about in the darkness.

Years after Micah's time, the prophet Jeremiah, with his life on the line, referred to elders who defended his prophetic ministry as he quoted from Micah 3:12: (Jeremiah 26:18)

> Micah of Moresheth prophesied in the days of Hezekiah king of Judah, and said to all the people of Judah: "Thus says the Lord of hosts, 'Zion shall be plowed as a field; Jerusalem shall become a heap of ruins, and the mountain of the house a wooded height.' "

These elders went on to point out that Micah's preaching had an impact on King Hezekiah and had stayed God's judgment upon the nation. They argued that, like Micah, Jeremiah spoke in the name of the Lord, and that his life should be spared. And it was.

In Micah's day, in Jeremiah's day, and in our day, there are those who recognize God's Word and appreciate the people who proclaim it.

5 The Burden of Leadership

In Luke 12:48, our Lord Jesus says, "Everyone to whom much was given, of him much will be required." When people are in positions of authority, much is expected of them. God through Micah has pointed to the spiritual and political leaders of His ancient people. God's expectations and warnings, however, are not limited to the ancient past.

Much of what is happening in the world today can be traced to godless leaders. It is especially tragic that so many in positions of authority within churches have given in to the trends in secular society instead of standing against those trends. Church leaders have caved in on matters of doctrine—saying, for instance, that the opening chapter of the Bible is compatible with the theory of evolution. They have caved on matters of practice—failing to distinguish, for instance, the God-given callings of men and women and how they differ. They have caved on matters of lifestyle—allowing and all the more so promoting same-sex marriages, even though Scripture does not condone this. It is not surprising, then, that so many Christians have become disillusioned with the church, with many leaving it entirely.

James, a brother of Jesus, wrote concerning the great responsibility of teaching within the church: (James 3:1) "Not many of you should become teachers, my brothers, for you know that we who teach will be judged with greater strictness." It is an extremely serious matter to depart from the clear teachings of God's Word.

God does not call minsters and teachers in the church to cater to the trends and desires of the times in which they live. The moral Law does not change from one generation to the next. In each generation, God calls leaders to be faithful to His Word. In regard to the public ministry, the apostle Paul wrote, (1 Corinthians 4:2–3) "Moreover, it is required of stewards that they be found faithful. But with me it is a very small thing that I should be judged by you or by any human court. In fact, I do not even judge myself." Ultimately, we answer to God alone.

While leadership has its responsibilities and carries with it a burden, it is also a privilege to proclaim God's saving message, as did the prophet Micah.

Conclusion

The idea of the remnant is a theme that runs through Scripture. In this world, believers are outnumbered. Jesus says, (Matthew 7:14) "For the gate is narrow and the way is hard that leads to life, and those who find it are few."

When we think of this reality, we can become discouraged, but this is not why God speaks of the remnant. God's Word simply tells the truth—that's the way it is in this fallen world. God wants us to stand firm in the faith not because everyone else is doing it but because it is the gate to heaven. Are we part of a remnant? Yes. Are we alone? Never. There are others with us in the struggle. Above all, God is with us, and "if God is for us, who can be against us?" (Romans 8:31). Nothing and no one can separate us from His love in Jesus Christ. No, we are never alone.

Concluding Activities

Conclude the session with an appropriate prayer and distribute the study leaflet for week 7.

Walk in the Name of the Lord

Micah 4–5

Preparing for the Session

Central Focus

God is faithful. Through the holy prophets, He made promises in the Old Testament that found their fulfillment in Jesus Christ in the New Testament; His Word is always sure, and it never fails.

Objectives

That participants, led by the Holy Spirit working through God's Word, will

1. patiently await the accomplishment of God's plans;
2. compare Old Testament prophecies with New Testament fulfillment; and
3. walk more closely with the Lord.

Note for the small-group leaders: Lesson notes and other materials you will need begin on page 67.

For the Lecture Leader

Session Plan

Worship

Begin the session with the hymn printed in the study leaflet. Accompaniments are available in denominational hymnals, such as *Lutheran Service Book* or *Lutheran Worship* (refer to hymnal index). (Note: Concordia Publishing House has available *The Concordia Organist.* All the initial worship hymns in the LifeLight courses are included in this resource. It's especially helpful for mission congregations and small parishes. See the list of study resources on p. 7.) Follow with this prayer:

Prayer

In keeping with Your promise, O Lord, from the little town of Bethlehem, the Ruler of Israel and of all creation has come forth. May the ends of the earth turn to Him and live! Uplift us by the certainty of Your Word, and strengthen our faith in our Savior, Jesus Christ, Your Son, our Lord, who lives and reigns with You and the Holy Spirit, one God, now and forever. Amen.

Lecture Presentation

Introduction

Apart from the famous passage identifying Bethlehem as the birthplace of the Messiah, most students of the Bible would probably be hard pressed to come up with anything else from Micah 4–5. Nevertheless, as will soon become evident, these two chapters might be seen as a summary of all of Scripture. The two chapters contain strong passages of Law and Gospel, messianic prophecy, assurance of God's deliverance from those who would destroy us, and even a glimpse of heaven.

1 Mount Zion *(4:1–5)*

The first five verses of Micah 4 are fascinating for several reasons. For one thing, they stand in stark contrast to the preceding chapters, which as we have seen, contain strong pronouncements of judgment upon unbelief; the verses before us now present the sweetest preachment of the Gospel in contrast to the terrifying proclamation of God's Law. Second, these verses have intrigued Bible students through the ages because they run parallel, almost word for word, to the opening verses of Isaiah 2; they raise the question of who borrowed from whom. Finally, these verses offer a sublime prophecy of the day when all nations will be joined together in perfect harmony; in other words, they point to heaven. We'll look at these three features.

The world in which we live offers daily confirmation of the fall into sin and its consequences. What God described in Genesis 3 is acted out in countless ways by all of humanity, and that includes us. People turn against one another even as they turn from God. Original sin is not a term used in the Bible, but it is a term that theologians use to describe the reality that sin and guilt pass from one generation to another. God's righteous judgment—"you shall surely die"—also passes onto all, for all have sinned. When individuals and nations harden themselves against God, they reap the whirlwind of destruction in this world and the world to come.

After his harsh, realistic preachment of God's Law, Micah is directed by the Holy Spirit to paint a new picture:

> The mountain of the house of the LORD shall be established . . . and peoples shall flow to it, . . . to the house of the God of Jacob, that He may teach us His ways . . . and they shall beat their swords into plowshares . . . and no one shall make them afraid.

Here we have a wonderful Gospel promise. There are no conditions attached, no demands or threats. God simply says that this is the way it will be.

The image of beating swords into plowshares is one of Scripture's best-known metaphors. Warfare gives way to peaceful, productive pursuits. Many seek this today. The Bible urges us to live peaceably with others, but perfect harmony will not be found this side of heaven.

Micah 4:1–5 closely parallels Isaiah 2:1–5 (see the comments on Obadiah 1–9 and Jeremiah 49 in Session 1). A look at the first two verses of each chapter will show just how close they are. [Presenter, the passages are included here for your convenience. You need not read them aloud to participants.]

> It shall come to pass in the latter days
> that the mountain of the house of the LORD
> shall be established as the highest of the mountains,
> and it shall be lifted up above the hills;
> and peoples shall flow to it,
> and many nations shall come, and say:
> "Come, let us go up to the mountain of the LORD,
> to the house of the God of Jacob,
> that He may teach us His ways
> and that we may walk in His paths."
> For out of Zion shall go forth the law,
> and the word of the LORD from Jerusalem.
> (Micah 4:1–2)

> It shall come to pass in the latter days
> that the mountain of the house of the LORD
> shall be established as the highest of the mountains,
> and shall be lifted up above the hills;
> and all the nations shall flow to it,
> and many peoples shall come, and say:
> "Come, let us go up to the mountain of the LORD,
> to the house of the God of Jacob,
> that He may teach us His ways
> and that we may walk in His paths."
> For out of Zion shall go the law,
> and the word of the Lord from Jerusalem.
> (Isaiah 2:1–2)

As you read these, you may wish to make a more in-depth, word-for-word comparison of the two parallel passages.

Micah and Isaiah were contemporaries. Did they know each other personally? Did they consult? If they did, it would not detract from the doctrine of the inspiration of Scripture, since one would simply build upon the other's work, just as writers in the New Testament quote and comment on the Old Testament. Elsewhere in Scripture, Luke tells us that he consulted and even did research for the writing of his Gospel: (Luke 1:2–3) "Just as those who from the beginning were eyewitnesses and ministers of the word have delivered them to us, it seemed good to me also, having followed all things closely for some time past, to write an orderly account." Similarities among the first three Gospels (the so-called Synoptic Gospels—Matthew, Mark, Luke) suggest borrowing or perhaps a common source. But whether giving an eyewitness account, a historical detail, or a prophecy of things to come, the holy writers were guided by the Holy Spirit in each case.

As for Isaiah and Micah, it has been suggested that Micah may have written just a few years earlier than Isaiah. But this is not known for certain. The parallel sections do have some variations, yet are in places word for word. They are not speaking of historical facts, which both prophets might have checked into or witnessed. They are speaking of the future. Perhaps the best suggestion is that God inspired both of them with the wording independently from each other.

In any case, this beautiful scene foretold by the ancient prophets will only unfold at Christ's second coming, for until then there will be "wars and rumors of wars" (Matthew 24:6). Years after Micah, the prophet Daniel would speak of a mountain that would fill "the whole earth" and that "shall never be destroyed" (Daniel 2:35, 44). This is "the mountain of the LORD" of which Micah speaks; it is the everlasting reign of the Messiah. It is for all nations, as Paul declares, (Romans 10:11–12) "For there is no distinction between Jew and Greek; for the same Lord is Lord of all, bestowing His riches on all who call on Him. For 'everyone who calls on the name of the Lord will be saved.'" The peace of which Micah speaks is not—as many have taken it—a political earthly peace among the nations. Rather, it is peace with God through Jesus Christ, who tells us, (John 14:27) "Peace I leave with you; My peace I give to you. Not as the world gives do I give to you. Let not your hearts be troubled, neither let them be afraid."

Micah, then, is pointing ahead to the distant future when paradise shall be restored. In the next chapter, he will point us to the one who will open the gates to heaven, the Messiah, Jesus, the Christ. We can revel in this beautiful depiction of what lies ahead for us because the Lord promises it. Just as God delivered on His promise to send the Savior into the world, He will also deliver on this promise of paradise. Micah declares that "we will walk in the name of the LORD our God forever and ever." Heaven is forever. It's also a sure thing, in Micah's words, "for the mouth of the Lord of hosts has spoken."

2 The Kingdom Restored to Zion *(4:6–13)*

"In that day," like the expression "in the latter days" in verse 1, is commonly used in the prophetic writings. It points ahead to the time when the Lord fulfills His promises of judgment and salvation. Until that time, the people of God must struggle—indeed, the whole world is in a state of pain. It is like "a woman in labor." The pains of childbirth are extreme, but after that comes the joy of a new God-given life entering the world.

Micah prophesies about gathering the afflicted, making the lame into a remnant, and making those who were cast off into a strong nation, with the Lord Himself ruling over them "from this time forth and forevermore." This is messianic and finds its fulfillment in the coming Savior. Jesus reaches out to the needy, the despised, and the lowly—to sinners who recognize their sinfulness, helplessness, spiritual poverty, and need for Christ. When Martin Luther died, a slip of paper was found in his pocket on which he had written, "We are beggars, this is true." Before the righteous and omnipotent God, none of us has anything to offer. Yet in Christ, we have everything. He has given His sinless life for us and conquered death so that we shall reign with Him forever. (Matthew 11:28) "Come to Me, all who labor and are heavy laden," Jesus says, "and I will give you rest."

Micah's mention here of Babylon is the only such mention in the entire book. It is a prophecy of the seventy-year captivity in Babylon: "Writhe and groan, O daughter of Zion . . . you shall go to Babylon." The Babylonian captivity lay more than a century in the future when the prophets Micah and Isaiah foretold it. In their day, Babylon was not yet the superpower it would become. Assyria, with its capital of Nineveh, was the empire of the day, dominating the ancient world. Yet Nineveh would fall to the Babylonians in 612, and Jerusalem would fall in 587 BC.

The name Zion appears five times in these verses, and three of the occurrences are prefaced with "daughter of." Zion, of course, was the name of one of the hills of Jerusalem, and it became another name for the city itself, the site of the temple of the Lord, which represented God's presence among His people. Even before King David made Jerusalem his capital, the site was referred to as "the stronghold of Zion" (2 Samuel 5:7). In poetic language, the prophets at times referred to Jerusalem as "daughter of Zion" (as here and, for example, Psalm 9:14). Beyond that, Jerusalem and Zion represent not just a physical place, but God's people and their eternal dwelling place in heaven. "Then I looked," says St. John in his vision of heaven, "and behold, on Mount Zion stood the Lamb" (Revelation 14:1). This is the eternal home of Jesus, the Lamb of God, and His people.

Though "many nations are assembled against" Zion, "they do not know the thoughts of the LORD." God's wisdom transcends all human understanding. In spite of the world's hatred and opposition, the Almighty watches over and protects Zion.

3 The Shepherd Prophecy *(5:1–5a)*

"O little town of Bethlehem, How still we see thee lie!" Perhaps the lovely Christmas carol brings memories of Christmas Eve from days past; memories of putting on winter coats and mittens to head to church for the children's service, memories of sitting by a warm fireplace and listening to this and other songs of the season, or—whether in a cold or more temperate climate—memories of singing the Christmas songs we love with family and friends.

We now sing the song two millennia after the first Christmas. And seven centuries before the birth of the Savior, Micah saw the same event: "But you, O Bethlehem Ephrathah, who are too little to be among the clans of Judah, from you shall come forth for Me one who is to be ruler in Israel." Ephrathah was one of the clans of the tribe of Judah, a minor clan by all estimates—except in God's eyes. From this town and region, a mere five miles south of the great city of Jerusalem, came the family of Elimelech and his wife, Naomi (Ruth 1:1–5). The couple took up residence during a time of famine in the neighboring country of Moab. There, the sons married Moabite women, one of whom was named Ruth.

To make a somewhat long story short, Ruth and Naomi were both widowed and returned to Bethlehem. There, Ruth married a man by the name of Boaz. From their line would come the most illustrious of the kings of Israel, David—slayer of Goliath, writer of almost half of the Bible's Psalms, epic in his conquests and in his sins, father of wise King Solomon—who was the ancestor of the King of kings and Lord of lords. From little Bethlehem came Jesus.

Jesus is described by Micah as the ruler "whose coming forth is from of old, from ancient days." Jesus is the eternal Son of the Father and could say to His challengers, (John 8:58) "Before Abraham was, I am." From Bethlehem would come the one of whom His disciple John wrote, (John 1:1, 14) "In the beginning was the Word, and the Word was with God, and the Word was God. . . . And the Word became flesh and dwelt among us." From little Bethlehem, the Ruler of the universe chose to enter the world in human flesh and blood.

The people of the land would go through many hardships ("he shall give them up") until "she who is in labor [Mary] has given birth." Micah proceeds to describe Jesus as the one who will "shepherd His flock." Jesus said of Himself, (John 10:14) "I am the good shepherd." He would stand in the majesty and strength of the Lord God omnipotent. Today, the name of Christ is praised around the world, with a third of the earth's population at least bearing the name Christian. From little Bethlehem would come He who would be "great to the ends of the earth."

And, says Micah, "He shall be their peace." Through His sacrificial death on the cross for our sins, Jesus brings us peace with God. The song "O Little Town of Bethlehem" continues:

> For Christ is born of Mary, And, gathered all above
> While mortals sleep, the angels keep Their watch of wond'ring love.
> O morning stars, together Proclaim the holy birth,
> And praises sing to God the king And peace to all the earth!

4 Assyrian Invasion *(5:5b–6)*

When Micah wrote these words, the invasion of the land of Judah was close at hand. During Micah's lifetime, mighty Assyria took Samaria, the capital of the Northern Kingdom of Israel, and carried the people into captivity. Then the Assyrians turned toward the Southern Kingdom of Judah, with its capital of Jerusalem. The armies of Assyria were known for their fierceness, and the very thought of them inspired fear. It was, for example, their practice to put the heads of their enemies on spikes as a warning to all who might dare try to oppose them.

Under King Sennacherib, they besieged the holy city in 701 BC: (2 Kings 18:13–17) "In the fourteenth year of King Hezekiah, Sennacherib king of Assyria came up against all the fortified cities of Judah and took them. . . . And they [Sennacherib's forces] went up and came to Jerusalem." But God miraculously turned back the seemingly unstoppable Assyrians, even as Micah foretold: "He shall deliver us from the Assyrian." As the Assyrians surrounded Jerusalem, God reassured Judah's king and people: (2 Kings 19:34) "I will defend this city to save it."

And save it He did! The "angel of the Lord went out and struck down 185,000 in the camp of the Assyrians. . . . Then Sennacherib king of Assyria departed and went home and lived at Nineveh" (2 Kings 19:35–36). Powerful armies and superpowers are not the ultimate source of our confidence. Rather, it is in the Lord of hosts, the almighty God who rules the nations and counts them as but dust on the scales. In the words of Isaiah, (40:22–23) "It is He who sits above the circle of the earth, . . . who brings princes to nothing, and makes the rulers of the earth as emptiness."

The English Romantic poet Lord Byron (1788–1824) captured this event in dramatic fashion in his poem "The Destruction of Sennacherib":

> The Assyrian came down like the wolf on the fold,
> And his cohorts were gleaming in purple and gold;
> And the sheen of their spears was like stars on the sea,
> When the blue wave rolls nightly on deep Galilee.
>
> Like the leaves of the forest when Summer is green,
> That host with their banners at sunset were seen:
> Like the leaves of the forest when Autumn hath blown,
> That host on the morrow lay withered and strown.
>
> For the Angel of Death spread his wings on the blast,
> And breathed in the face of the foe as he passed;
> And the eyes of the sleepers waxed deadly and chill,
> And their hearts but once heaved, and for ever grew still!

At times, we may become fearful when we consider the many threats that surround us, our community, and our nation. Yet, as always, God is in control.

5 A Remnant Shall Be Delivered *(5:7–15)*

The term "remnant" is frequently used in the Bible. It speaks of those who remain after most of the people have been lost or destroyed. Although the Assyrians took into captivity the ten tribes of the Northern Kingdom of Israel, a "remnant . . . escaped from the hand of the kings of Assyria" (2 Chronicles 30:6). Elsewhere, it refers to those who escaped the destruction at the hands of the Babylonians, survived the exile in Babylon, and returned to the land of Judah and city of Jerusalem (Haggai 1:12). It can also refer to the Jews scattered "among the nations, in the midst of many peoples," as in Micah 5:8.

Among its other uses, the term can describe those who remain faithful while the majority of people fall away from the Lord. Referring back to the prophet Isaiah, the apostle Paul declared, (Romans 9:27) "And Isaiah cries out concerning Israel: 'Though the number of the sons of Israel be as the sand of the sea, only a remnant of them will be saved.' "

The idea of the remnant has two sides to it. On the one hand, it is a warning lest we are tempted to go along with the crowd, as Jesus says, (Matthew 7:13–14) "Enter by the narrow gate. For the gate is wide and the way is easy that leads to destruction, and those who enter by it are many. For the gate is narrow and the way is hard that leads to life, and those who find it are few." On the other hand, it is comforting to know that God sees to it that He has His people. (Isaiah 1:9) "If the Lord of hosts had not left us a few survivors, we should have been like Sodom, and become like Gomorrah."

God promises to "root out your Asherah images" (some translations, "Asherah poles"). These were wooden posts in the images of the goddess Asherah, the fertility goddess and consort of the idol Baal, to whom so many of the people had turned as they forsook the true God. (See the discussion of Micah 6:9–16 in Session 8.) This goddess was worshiped amid groves of trees on hilltops (the "high places" of which the Bible speaks). During his reign, good King Josiah (640–609 BC) began to purge Judah of its idolatry, chopping down the altars of the Baals and breaking into pieces the Asherah images, also known as Asherim (2 Chronicles 34:1–7). Nevertheless, the lure of this goddess continued to plague the land until the people went into exile in Babylon.

The lure of sin is very strong; the devil, the world, and our own sinful flesh would all consort to pull us away from the Lord. Yet God is stronger and will deliver His people from their enemies, cut off the idolatry from among His people, and destroy those who oppose His plans. No matter how many fall away, God will keep His remnant.

Conclusion

Like the rest of Micah, chapters 4–5 are powerful pronouncements of God's judgment and His grace. These chapters also contain startling prophecies: (1) of the Assyrian invasion of Judah (5:5b–6), (2) of the Babylonian captivity of the Jews and their return from the exile (4:6–10), (3) of the coming of the Messiah, the Christ (5:2–5a), and (4) of the glories of heaven for God's people (4:1–5). Writing by divine inspiration, Micah and the other Old Testament literary prophets painted amazing pictures of what was to come.

These two wonderful chapters are reminders that God is always with us. He is there for us even in the most terrible times. Through Christ, we have that assurance: (Romans 8:31–32, 38–39)

> If God be for us, who can be against us? He who did not spare His own Son but gave Him up for us all, how will He not also with Him graciously give us all things? . . . For I am sure that neither death nor life, nor angels nor rulers, nor things present nor things to come, nor powers, nor height nor depth, nor anything else in all creation, will be able to separate us from the love of God in Christ Jesus our Lord.

Concluding Activities

Conclude the session with an appropriate prayer and distribute the study leaflet for week 8.

Walk Humbly with Your God

Micah 6

Preparing for the Session

Central Focus

Throughout history, the Lord has showered His people with blessings, and He will continue to be with us forever. Yet the history of those who have rejected Him serves as a warning against unbelief.

Objectives

That participants, led by the Holy Spirit working through God's Word, will

1. remember God's workings in the past;
2. understand that God's judgments are always just; and
3. practice justice and kindness toward others.

Note for the small-group leaders: Lesson notes and other materials you will need begin on page 69.

For the Lecture Leader

Session Plan

Worship

Begin the session with the hymn printed in the study leaflet. Accompaniments are available in denominational hymnals, such as *Lutheran Service Book* or *Lutheran Worship* (refer to hymnal index). (Note: Concordia Publishing House has available *The Concordia Organist.* All the initial worship hymns in the LifeLight courses are included in this resource. It's especially helpful for mission congregations and small parishes. See the list of study resources on p. 7.) Follow with this prayer:

Prayer

O Lord God almighty, we bow before You in worship, thankful for Your countless gifts of grace. Forgive our sins, renew us, strengthen us, and guide us so that we may daily serve You by doing justice, loving kindness, and walking humbly with You. We ask this through Jesus Christ, Your Son, our Lord, who lives and reigns with You and the Holy Spirit, one God, now and forever. Amen.

Lecture Presentation

Introduction

In chapter 5, Micah has spoken of "the remnant of Jacob" that God would keep amid the nations. God continues with a reminder of His care for the chosen people, while at the same time indicting the people for their sins. Micah 6 might be seen as an evaluation of the state of the nation. As will be evident, in spite of God's care, the nation was not in a healthy condition. It had followed the worst leaders and given itself over to false gods.

Although God—through devoted prophets like Micah—urged the people to "remember" what He did for them, they persisted in forgetting. Such willful wickedness would bring God's punishment.

1 Indictment against God's People *(6:1–5)*

Like Micah 1:2 and 3:1, this section also begins with a call to "Hear." God calls on the people to "plead your case." He is the Judge, and the people are on trial. The courtroom is not inside a building, but all of nature stands as a jury: "Hear, you mountains, the indictment of the LORD . . . against His people."

God reminds the people how He had delivered them from Egypt, "from the house of slavery," with Moses and his brother and sister—Aaron and Miriam—to lead them. In guiding them to the Promised Land, God showered them with goodness.

As they journeyed through the wilderness on their way to the land God had sworn to their father Abraham, the people were protected by their Lord. "Remember what Balak king of Moab devised." This king had wanted to destroy God's people, and he had even hired a pagan diviner, Balaam, to curse the Israelites. Yet even after offering sacrifices to idols, when Balaam opened his mouth, he could only bless them!

God went on to remind the people of "what happened from Shittim to Gilgal." Shittim was their last stop in the journey through the desert; Gilgal was their first stop in the Promised Land. This marked a period of transition from journey to destination, from anticipation to fulfillment.

All this looking back was so that they might "know the saving acts of the Lord." God has revealed His salvation in the past; He says to His people through the ages, "Remember." His faithfulness and love will never change.

2 God and History

The brief review of past blessings that God presented through Micah was not unusual. The Prophets and Writings are replete with such historical sketches. Following the Pentateuch (Genesis through Deuteronomy), the rest of the Old Testament is a continual building upon this foundation, with frequent references to the great events and outstanding characters of the first five books of Scripture. Chief among those events are the creation and the exodus. Chief among the people are Abraham and Moses.

Actually, this pattern does not end with the Old Testament but continues into the New. There, Jesus and the apostles continue to hark back to the foundations. For example, alluding to Moses and naming Abraham, Jesus identified Himself as the Lord who appeared to Moses in the burning bush (see Exodus 3) and in whom Abraham rejoiced (see John 8:56).

In those foundational Scriptures, the Lord set the pattern for all that was to follow: mankind's sin, God's judgment, God's promises, and the fulfillment of deliverance. This was the beginning of history, and God's people are to be students of history.

Christianity is a historical faith. This is not simply saying it began at a certain time in history; that could be said of any religion. It is historic in that it recounts God's dealings with the world throughout history. Scripture is not simply telling myths, like the Bhagavad Gita tells the story of Krishna; it is not simply making laws, like the Qur'an's many demands to do this or that in the name of Allah. The Bible's stories are true and its commands, like its promises, come from the Lord of history, who has intervened in human events and directs the course of history to carry out His gracious plans.

The people of the Bible were real flesh-and-blood human beings—not invented mythological characters. They are connected to times and places—sometimes quite specifically, as was the case with the prophet Micah or the apostle Paul.

The places of the Bible are real, identifiable places; for example, Dr. Paul Maier has noted that the Book of Acts and the Letters of Paul correctly describe the locations and places named for the missionary travels of St. Paul. While not every single place mentioned in the Bible has been accurately confirmed, the vast majority of the many, many locations has been established.

The events of the Bible were real. The fall of Jerusalem to the Babylonians, prophesied and spoken of in the Old Testament, took place. The fall of Jerusalem to the Romans, foretold in the New Testament, took place.

Even beyond biblical people, places, and events, we can see God's hand in all of history. Nations rise and fall, as God raises them up, weighs them, and brings them down: (Isaiah 40:15) "Behold, the nations are like a drop from a bucket, and are accounted as the dust on the scales." God wants us to be students of history, beginning with Bible history and expanding into the unfolding of world events.

Luther had a deep interest in history and spoke highly of its value as we see in it God's hand. He commented:

> Histories are nothing else than indications, memorials, and tokens of divine works and judgments, informing us how God sustains, rules, checks, furthers, punishes, and honors the world, especially people, as each one deserves evil or good. And though there are many who neither recognize nor regard God, yet they cannot but be painfully aware of these examples and histories and fear that they, too, will fare like this and that man described by history. This moves them more strongly than the effort of people to check them and to keep them from doing wrong by mere words or by teaching them what is right. (*WLS* § 1999)

Above all, for Christians, the study of history is a reminder of God's faithfulness to His people. In history—in "the fullness of time"—God sent His Son into the world to save it (Galatians 4:4). The Lord watches over and guides believers through the most terrible times. Sir Isaac Watts (1674–1748), the "Father of English Hymnody," captured the confidence we can have for the future as we consider God's help in the past:

> O God, our help in ages past,
> Our hope for years to come,
> Our shelter from the stormy blast,
> And our eternal home.

3 What Does the Lord Require? *(6:6–8)*

God has recounted His past goodness to His chosen people. And now, what does the Lord look for in return? Does He look for "burnt offerings," "thousands of rams," or "ten thousands of rivers of oil," or even—God forbid—the offering of the "firstborn"?

It is not the outward ceremonies that God looks for, but He seeks a change of heart. As the psalmist David put it, (Psalm 51:17) "The sacrifices of God are a broken spirit; a broken and contrite heart, O God, You will not despise." Through Micah, God declares, (6:8) "[The Lord] has told you, O man, what is good; and what does the LORD require of you but to do justice, and to love kindness, and to walk humbly with your God?"

This is a message that rings across the ages and down to our own. We find it easy to go through the motions of religion: going to church, putting something in the collection plate, standing, sitting, singing the hymns. All of that is good, just as the offering of the ancient sacrifices was. But God looks to the heart of each one of us.

4 Destruction of the Wicked *(6:9–16)*

This last section of Micah 6 is a strong denunciation of the wicked and their wickedness. In spite of God's deliverance and love, the people persisted in their wickedness. "The city" is decried because the sins enumerated here were more common to urban life: dishonest business practices (false scales and weights), violence, and deceit.

Because of their wickedness, God threatens punishment. As with the sins, the punishments are enumerated: the inability to find satisfaction, lack of results from their labors, desolation, and scorn. At times, the wicked prosper in this life, only to receive their just rewards in the life to come. Often, however, it is the case that punishment comes already in the here and now. This seems to be the case especially when there is collective guilt, when an entire society gives itself over to godlessness. Civilizations fall when their cup of iniquity overflows (see Genesis 15:16).

At times we hear people say (perhaps we've said it as well) that God hates sin but loves the sinner. That is not quite accurate, for the Bible says that God does actually hate sinners: (Psalm 5:5–6) "The boastful shall not stand before Your [God's] eyes; You hate all evildoers. You destroy those who speak lies; the LORD abhors the bloodthirsty and deceitful man." God's hatred for sinners and His love for sinners seem contradictory; they can only be reconciled in the cross of Christ. There Jesus suffered God's hatred for sinners and at the same time demonstrated God's love for sinners. Aside from Christ, we can never hope to stand in the presence of the holy God.

In the closing verse of this chapter, the Lord sarcastically commends the wicked nation for keeping the "statutes [laws] of Omri, and all the work of the house of Ahab," two of the most notorious kings of Israel.

Only eight verses of 1 Kings deal with Omri's reign (885–874 BC). He had been commander of the army and came to royal power during a time of civil unrest (the previous king, Zimri, had reigned for only seven days!). Omri proved himself a capable ruler, establishing the capital of Israel in Samaria, keeping peace with Judah to the south, and conquering Moab. Nevertheless, he allowed the worship of the Canaanite god Baal to be practiced alongside that of the Lord, Yahweh. The Bible's assessment of Omri is blunt: (1 Kings 16:25) "Omri did what was evil in the sight of the LORD, and did more evil than all who were before him." What ultimately counts is not worldly success but one's relationship with God.

If Omri did more evil than those who preceded him, his son Ahab would soon break his record. Like Omri, Ahab (874–853 BC) proved himself a capable ruler but a wicked influence on his nation. In order to form an alliance with the country of Phoenicia, Omri had arranged the marriage of his son to the daughter of the Phoenician King Ethbaal (meaning "man of Baal"). Ahab and Jezebel have gone down as one of history's most infamous couples. With Ahab's approbation, Jezebel promoted the building of a temple to Baal in Samaria, supported hundreds of priests and prophets of Baal, and came into bitter conflict with the great prophet Elijah. The Bible has several chapters that deal with Ahab and describe him as above and beyond his father in wickedness: (1 Kings 16:33) "And Ahab made an Asherah [fertility idol of the Canaanites and consort of Baal]. Ahab did more to provoke the LORD, the God of Israel, to anger than all the kings of Israel who were before him."

As for the idol Baal, the worship of whom led the people away from Yahweh, this was the god of the people who lived among the Israelites. Baal was the god of rain and thunder, and consequently of the fertility that water brings to the land. The name Baal means "lord" or "master" and has been joined with zebub, which means "flies"; Baalzebub (or Beelzebub) is a name of Satan, the Lord of the Flies; that is, the lord of the garbage heap, of all that is filthy and disgusting. For example, the worship of Baal involved child sacrifice and temple prostitution.

So Omri and Ahab have become the two role models, says Micah, "and you have walked in their counsels." The people were tempted by the alluring rituals of idol worship, at times trying to compromise it with the worship of the Lord, and at times not even making the attempt to hide it. The result? God would make them "a desolation" and "a hissing." The people would be devastated and brought low; they would be scorned—hissed at and mocked.

Reading this passage, it is hard to escape the parallels with modern society, in which down the street from the church is the allure of the world with its shiny idols. No farther removed than a smartphone, radio, or television, the world beckons with the promise of self-indulgence and pleasure. Yet, in the end, those who reject God's grace will bring upon themselves destruction. In God's message from Micah, we see Him threatening the wicked, both then and now, with desolation "because of your sins."

5 The Proper Distinction between Law and Gospel

There is a time for declaring the Law and a time for preaching the Gospel. In the Book of Micah, we have seen both—and we will in the final chapter as well. On the one hand, Micah presents powerful passages denouncing sin and threatening judgment. On the other hand, he declares God's forgiveness, deliverance, and salvation.

These two doctrines—the Law and the Gospel—run throughout the entire Bible, and to understand the distinction between them is a key element in understanding all of Scripture. In his treatise on the Proper Distinction between Law and Gospel, C. F. W. Walther (1811–77) spoke to future pastors concerning the use of both:

> A sermon that does not contain any Law is worthless. In every gathering of people there are always some impenitent persons who must be shocked out of their sleep of sin. . . . For the Law passes judgment on sinners. However, God did not send His Son to pass judgment on the world, but to save the world through Him. By the term *world* the Lord refers to mankind in its apostate and lost condition—made up of the lost, accursed, and condemned sinners. To these the Savior brings this blessed doctrine: "Even though you have broken every commandment of God, do not despair; I am bringing you forgiveness and salvation now and forevermore." (*Law and Gospel: How to Read and Apply the Bible* [St. Louis: Concordia Publishing House, 2010], Theses 2 and 5, pp. 45, 83)

While not difficult to distinguish between the two in theory, to know when and how to apply them is an art, as Luther noted,

> But everything depends on the proper differentiation of these two messages and on not mixing them together; otherwise one will know and retain the proper understanding of neither the one nor the other; nay, while under the impression of having both, one will have neither. . . . Therefore place the man who is able nicely to divorce the Law from the Gospel at the head of the list and call him a Doctor of Holy Scripture, for without the Holy Spirit the attainment of this differentiating is impossible. (*WLS* § 2276)

Throughout the Book of Micah, the divinely inspired prophet weaves back and forth between the two. He proclaims judgment and destruction upon the hardened people who had turned from God to idols. He reassures the poor in spirit by reminding them of God's past blessings. This pattern will continue to the end of the book, which concludes with a magnificent Gospel declaration of God's steadfast love.

Conclusion

As we reflect on the history of God's Old Testament people, we see so much of ourselves there. Although separated from their world by almost three millennia, by thousands of miles, and by language and customs, we share the same tendency to drift away from God and toward evil. We need the same reminders of God's goodness throughout our past and of His promises of future deliverance.

The terms *justice*, *mercy*, and *grace* often come up in regard to God's dealings with human beings. *Justice* can be defined as "getting what we deserve," and *mercy* can be defined as "not getting what we deserve." *Grace* is in a class by itself, for by God's grace we get what we do not deserve. God showers upon us His undeserved gifts of love, forgiveness of sins, salvation, and eternal life.

All of this comes through Jesus Christ, the promised Messiah of the Old Testament and the Savior of the human race. When we consider all the priceless treasures God continues to bless us with, we humbly thank our gracious God.

Concluding Activities

Conclude the session with an appropriate prayer and distribute the study leaflet for week 9.

When I Fall, I Shall Rise

Micah 7

Preparing for the Session

Central Focus

Despite human sin and failing, God's plan of salvation triumphs in the end. His steadfast love endures forever, for Jesus Christ is the Savior who has won for this fallen world its salvation.

Objectives

That participants, led by the Holy Spirit working through God's Word, will

1. daily repent of their sins, confident in God's grace;
2. wait for God's answers to their needs and prayers; and
3. rejoice in God's salvation in Christ.

Note for the small-group leaders: Lesson notes and other materials you will need begin on page 71.

For the Lecture Leader

Session Plan

Worship

Begin the session with the hymn printed in the study leaflet. Accompaniments are available in denominational hymnals, such as *Lutheran Service Book* or *Lutheran Worship* (refer to hymnal index). (Note: Concordia Publishing House has available *The Concordia Organist*. All the initial worship hymns in the LifeLight courses are included in this resource. It's especially helpful for mission congregations and small parishes. See the list of study resources on p. 7.) Follow with this prayer:

Prayer

Who is a God like You, O Lord, pardoning iniquity and passing over transgression? Our hearts overflow with joy as we consider Your compassion, faithfulness, and steadfast love! Be with us now and throughout this life, until we join the saints in heaven above to praise You, through Jesus Christ, Your Son, our Lord, who lives and reigns with You and the Holy Spirit, one God, now and forever. Amen.

Lecture Presentation

Introduction

The final chapter of Micah serves as a powerful conclusion to our study of Obadiah, Jonah, and Micah. Here again, we see a dynamic preachment of the Law of God, with its threats and punishments, alongside the Gospel, with its promises and deliverance. The book ends with a triumphant statement of God's steadfast love to His people.

It was in ancient Greece, a couple of centuries after the time of Micah, that the theater and drama were born. There were (and remain) two basic types of drama: tragedies and comedies. Tragedies involve sad endings but carry with them a lesson. Unlike the modern idea of comedy, which often brings to mind uproarious laughter, the essential idea of a comedy involves a story with a happy ending. That is the meaning of the term in Dante Alighieri's (1265–1321) epic poem *The Divine Comedy*, which ends in *paradiso*, in heaven.

Considered in that light, although the Bible contains much that is tragic, it is the quintessential divine comedy. It does not end with paradise lost but with paradise regained. The Book of Micah also ends on a triumphant note of the victory of God's love—just as do the prophecies of Obadiah and Jonah. The essential message of Scripture is God's victory over sin, death, and the devil. Indeed, Scripture is God's record of victory—of grace over sin, love over hatred, joy over sorrow, life over death, and heaven over hell. All of this comes through the Son of God, Jesus Christ.

1 Micah's Lament *(7:1–7)*

"Woe is me!" exclaims the prophet, as he looks in vain for a godly person. But, says Micah, it's like looking for grain or fruit after the harvest. The philosopher Blaise Pascal (1623–62) noted, "There are only two kinds of men: the righteous who believe they are sinners, and the sinners who believe they are righteous." It is often the case that ungodly people think very highly of themselves and their goodness, while the truly righteous acknowledge their unworthiness before God. We might think of the story Jesus told of the self-righteous Pharisee who thanked God he was not like others, including the tax collector beside him in the temple. The latter, Jesus went on to say, bowed his head and pleaded, "God, be merciful to me, a sinner!" (Luke 18:13) and went home justified before God.

We might add that there is a third type of person—the one who never even seems to think about whether he is righteous. This person just pursues whatever desires come his or her way. Micah looks at the world around him and sees bloodshed and people out to take advantage of one another. Those who should lead and set examples—the prince and the judge—take bribes. Even the person looked upon as "the great man" is bent on evil.

The "best of them" and the "most upright of them" (note the poetic parallelism) are like briers and thorn hedges. Confusion takes over, and even the distinction between mere civility and unbridled selfishness evaporates. This is "the day of your watchmen." The day of judgment foretold by the prophets of God "has come."

When wickedness reigns, no one is to be trusted: neighbors, friends, spouses, children, in-laws. This sorry state of affairs is not unlike our society today, in which people sacrifice relationships in the pursuit of self-interests.

Jesus uses this imagery when He says, (Luke 12:51–53)

> Do you think that I have come to give peace on earth? No, I tell you, but rather division. For from now on in one house there will be five divided, three against two and two against three. They will be divided, father against son and son against father, mother against daughter and daughter against mother, mother-in-law against her daughter-in-law and daughter-in-law against mother-in-law.

It is not that Jesus causes division, but sin does.

The Bible tells us not to place our trust in human beings and human relationships. Even the most powerful people are mortal. It's as the psalmist reminds us, (Psalm 146:3–4) "Put not your trust in princes, in a son of man, in whom there is no salvation. When his breath departs, he returns to the earth; on that very day his plans perish." The psalm goes on to show where we should place our confidence: (v. 5) "Blessed is he whose help is the God of Jacob, whose hope is in the LORD his God."

Micah continues, (7:7) "But as for me, I will look to the LORD." The body of believers consists of many people, yet ultimately each individual must speak for himself or herself. Micah's words are reminiscent of Joshua, when he gave his farewell to the people of Israel: (24:15)

> And if it is evil in your eyes to serve the LORD, choose this day whom you will serve, whether the gods your fathers served in the region beyond the River, or the gods of the Amorites in whose land you dwell. But as for me and my house, we will serve the LORD.

Steeped in the earlier Scriptures as he (like the other prophets) was, no doubt Micah had Joshua's words in mind.

Our trust must first rest in God, not in other people, no matter how close or how powerful they are. This is exactly what Micah will go on to say.

2 Confidence in the Lord's Deliverance *(7:8–17)*

Beginning with verse 8 and continuing through verse 10, Micah repeatedly uses the pronoun *I*, but he is no longer speaking just of himself. He is speaking on behalf of his fellow believers. Because their confidence was in the Lord, they could be sure that even if they fell they would rise again. They were ready to "bear the indignation of the LORD because I have sinned against Him." Believers are very much aware of their failings and daily confess their sins, sure of God's forgiveness.

Micah oscillates between the unbelievers being brought low and God's people being raised up. Although the proud and arrogant might ask, "Where is the LORD your God?" in the end, it is not the believers who are left low, but those who defy God and harass His people: "My eyes will look upon her; now she will be trampled down like the mire of the streets." Just as *I* represents the believers, *she* and *her* represent the enemies of God. Although unbelievers scoff at God's faithful people, their day will come.

In verse 11, Micah speaks of people from all over in ever-widening circles from Jerusalem—from Assyria to Egypt and to the River (a reference to the Euphrates River); from sea to sea, and from mountain to mountain. This parallels the opening chapter of the Book of Acts, where Jesus told His disciples that they would be His witnesses "in Jerusalem and in all Judea and Samaria, and to the end of the earth" (1:8).

While "the earth will be desolate because of its inhabitants," the people whom God shepherds will prosper "in Bashan and Gilead," fertile lands to the east of the Sea of Galilee and Jordan River. (Gilead was bordered on the north by Bashan and on the south by Moab.) Even the mighty of the world will be humbled—"they shall lick the dust like a serpent"—and "turn in dread to the LORD our God, and they shall be in fear of You." Those who stand opposed to God will be brought down, but Israel—that is, the people of God—will be raised up.

All of this finds its fulfillment in the messianic age, when every knee will bow before Jesus, "and every tongue confess that Jesus Christ is Lord" (Philippians 2:11).

3 Doxology of God's Mercy *(7:18–20)*

These closing verses of Micah are pure Gospel: God pardons iniquity, passes over transgression, does not retain His anger, delights in steadfast love, has compassion on us, casts our sins into the depths of the sea, and shows faithfulness and love.

As a prelude to these wonderful expressions of God's grace, Micah asks the rhetorical question "Who is a God like You?" The answer is, of course, no one. This is no mere wistful thinking, a vague wish that our God is somehow above the others. It is an assertion of bedrock fact. One can search through all the religions and philosophies of the world and not find a god like the God who has revealed Himself in Holy Scripture.

"Who is a God like You?" Look elsewhere and see if there is another. All but one of the Qur'an's 114 surahs (or chapters) begin, "In the name of Allah the beneficent, the merciful." Yet nowhere in those chapters do we find that beneficence and mercy; instead we find demands and threats and calls to do good. The sacred texts of the East speak of attaining release from this world into *nirvana* (also known as *moksha*). Yet those texts tell people to follow the way of devotion, or meditation, or works—good karma—to attain that end. The cults that seem to have sprung up everywhere point to this or that leader who alleges to show the way to God, and then those leaders call on disciples to earn their way by unswerving commitment to the cause. And the world's great philosophers talk of the way to a better world—if we adhere to their plan.

All of the world's religions and philosophies, outside of biblical Christianity, point to the way of works. Scripture alone points to grace.

"Who is a God like You?" There is none. The Lord's promises of forgiveness and salvation are backed up by action. God sent His Son, Jesus, into the world to live the perfect life God's Law demands and to suffer the punishment for breaking it that justice requires. This was the plan of salvation first uttered in Eden when Adam and Eve fell into sin and brought death into the world. God promised to crush the head of the serpent Satan. This is the promise "sworn to our fathers from the days of old" and fulfilled in the coming of Jesus Christ into the world. The Reformation hymnwriter Paul Speratus (1484–1551) summed it up beautifully:

> Salvation unto us has come
> By God's free grace and favor;
> Good works cannot avert our doom,
> They help and save us never.
> Faith looks to Jesus Christ alone,
> Who did for all the world atone;
> He is our one Redeemer.

To return to the expressions that Micah has used in describing God, we will note a few from this treasure chest. God is "pardoning iniquity"; God the Judge does not demand the punishment our sins deserve. He is "passing over transgression for the remnant." Looking ahead to the New Testament, the Lord put it this way: (Jeremiah 31:34) "For I will forgive their iniquity, and I will remember their sin no more."

He treads our iniquities underfoot, and He casts them into the depths of the sea; these are both dramatic metaphors that show how completely God eradicates our wrongdoings. He does this all for Jacob (Israel) and Abraham, who represent their spiritual descendants. Elsewhere, Abraham is designated as "the father of all who believe" (Romans 4:11). God's grace goes back to ancient times, back to eternity, and it extends into the future without end.

"God is love" (1 John 4:8, 16). That is His very nature. Punishment is, as Isaiah put it, God's "alien" work (Isaiah 28:21). He is much more desirous to forgive than to condemn: "where sin increased, grace abounded all the more" (Romans 5:20).

This closing to Micah's prophecy is a doxology, a word of praise. We can read it over and over without exhausting its riches. We can memorize the words and treasure them in our hearts. "Who is a God like You?" The Bible is replete with beautiful doxologies, as that of Romans 11:33–36: "Oh, the depth of the riches and wisdom and knowledge of God!"

Christian worship services often close with the singing of uplifting words of praise, such as this well-known doxology written by Thomas Ken (1637–1711):

> Praise God, from whom all blessings flow;
> Praise Him, all creatures here below;
> Praise Him above, ye heav'nly host:
> Praise Father, Son, and Holy Ghost.

4 Predictive Prophecy

As we near the end of our study on three of the Minor Prophets, a word is in order concerning the matter of predictive prophecy. If one reads through the numerous commentaries on these and the other Old Testament prophets, it becomes clear that many scholars—especially among more modern academics—do not believe that these writers could or did foretell the future.

We live in a humanistic age. That is, ours is a man-centered or human-centered age in which thinkers tend to put reason above revelation. Going back to the eighteenth-century Enlightenment, human reason has been extolled to the point where it is considered godlike. In 1793, during the French Revolution and spurred on by the Cult of Reason, an attempt was made to replace Christian faith with faith in Reason. In Notre Dame Cathedral in Paris, the Christian altar was replaced with an altar to liberty and reason, with the crowd paying homage to a woman who was to personify these values.

Such crass worship of Reason was relatively short-lived. Nevertheless, in most of the Western world since then, reason (also referred to as rationalism) has come to dominate academia, including much that is church affiliated. Bringing this back to our study of the Minor Prophets, it has become customary for commentators to explain away predictive prophecy: it is unreasonable. Prophecies—such as, for instance, Micah's prophecy regarding Bethlehem (Micah 5:2)—are said to have meant something other than what the New Testament writers took them to mean.

Of prophecies regarding events fulfilled within the Old Testament itself—for example, the Babylonian captivity (Micah 4:10)—another approach might well be used. It boils down to the argument that the prophecy was actually written after the event; either Micah lived later than was traditionally held, or that portion of his book was added later. The idea that the prophet Micah, inspired by God, actually foretold a coming event with such accuracy is not an option.

Bible-believing Christians hold that God in His wisdom and power is able to do all things, and that includes giving to His inspired prophets the words of things to come. This is above reason, although not really contrary to it. Why should not an omniscient and omnipotent God be able to carry this out? This is the position presented within the Bible itself.

And this was the position of Jesus Christ. After He rose from the dead, Jesus met two disciples who were walking from Jerusalem to the village of Emmaus. They were weighted heavy with disappointment and disillusionment. At first, they did not recognize Jesus as He walked alongside them, and they shared the sad events of His death. They reported that "some women of our company" had said that Jesus was alive (Luke 24:22–23).

Jesus then chided them for their lack of faith: (Luke 24:25–27)

> And He said to them, "O foolish ones, and slow of heart to believe all that the prophets have spoken! Was it not necessary that the Christ should suffer these things and enter into His glory?" And beginning with Moses and all the Prophets, He interpreted to them in all the Scriptures the things concerning Himself.

This was, and is, Jesus' response to those who reject the notion of predictive prophecy.

5 The Prophets for Today

The Old Testament prophets spoke as God's representatives. Jesus and the New Testament writers accepted their writings—along with the rest of the Old Testament Scriptures—as authoritative. The prophets spoke of events in their own times and prophesied of things to come, especially pointing to the coming of the Messiah. Jesus said that "the Scriptures . . . bear witness about Me" (John 5:39). And their timeless message continues to ring through the ages, applying to people everywhere.

From our study of three of the Minor Prophets, it is evident that their messages definitely apply in our day. The sins of *then* are the sins of *now*. God's judgment upon individuals and entire nations then is His judgment now. God's grace and forgiveness are the same today as then. The Savior they looked to in promise, we look back to in fulfillment. Granted, since Christ came, we are not bound to the Old Testament laws and ceremonies. Yet the faith and God's promises endure. He remains forever changeless: (Hebrews 13:8) "Jesus Christ is the same yesterday and today and forever."

Are we to expect more prophets? No. The story of salvation is complete—from God's first promise in Eden (Genesis 3:15), to the coming of the Savior, to His closing promise to come again "soon" (Revelation 22:20–21). It is not for us to await new revelations; rather, it remains for us to search the Scriptures and to carry out the Great Commission of preaching the Gospel to all creation.

Ultimately, the Scriptures focus on God's "steadfast love" in Jesus Christ. We see this in the prophets Obadiah, Jonah, Micah; we see it everywhere in the pages of Holy Writ. Through the prophet Jeremiah, the Lord declares to us as His people of old, (31:3) "I have loved you with an everlasting love."

Conclusion

Of the three Minor Prophets in this study guide, Micah is the longest. This book is also the one that focuses on the chosen people, rather than on a foreign nation or nations. And yet its focus is not narrow. Rather, the book is like a rich tapestry, sweeping in its scope. It is a masterpiece of history relating to the two kingdoms of Israel and, especially, Judah. It contains dark prophecies of impending doom upon sinful nations, contrasting with golden prophecies of messianic deliverance. Passages of judgment—the Law—weave in and out with passages of salvation—the Gospel. We see portraits of the people of Micah's day and their spiritual, social, and political leaders. We see ourselves, as Micah's inspired words speak across the ages to us: (6:8) "And what does the LORD require of you but to do justice, and to love kindness, and to walk humbly with your God?"

Above all, the Book of Micah points to Jesus Christ. Not only does it identify the place of His birth, but it also depicts the salvation that He would bring into the world. Through Him, our sins have been cast into the sea and washed away forever.

Concluding Activities

If possible, announce the next LifeLight course and encourage participants to register and invite others to participate also. Speak a prayer thanking God for the growth experienced during this course and for continued growth through His Word for all participants.

Small-Group Leaders Material

The Ghent Altarpiece (1425–32), Hubert van Eyck, detail. Iberfoto / Iberfoto

The Day of the Lord Is Near
Obadiah

Preparing for the Session

Central Focus

God's power and grace are seen in His reign on behalf of His people. He brings judgment upon those—like the Edomites—who reject Him, and He restores those who are His.

Objectives

That participants, led by the Holy Spirit working through God's Word, will

1. appreciate God's rule over all the nations;
2. stand in awe of God's judgments upon unrighteousness and unbelief; and
3. humbly trust God's grace toward His people.

For the Small-Group Leader

Small-Group Discussion Helps

Day 1 • Genesis 25:19–34 and Jeremiah 49:7–22

1. Edom, which was located between the Dead Sea and the Gulf of Aqaba during Old Testament times. Idumea, the New Testament name for the region of Edom, included the Negeb region south of Judea.

2. Edom, which sounds like the Hebrew word for "red," was a name for Esau, who was the older son of Isaac and Rebekah. So the Edomites were closely related to the Israelites.

3. The Lord proclaims a time of calamity and punishment for Edom. The nations would come against Edom, the nation would become small, it would be laid waste, and the people would be dragged away.

4. Obadiah and Jeremiah use very similar words, suggesting that their prophecies were written for the same or similar events. Since Jeremiah ministered at the time of the Babylonians, that would favor the c. 587–555 BC date for the Book of Obadiah.

5. (a) The prophet received a vision and heard a report from the Lord. (b) Obadiah saw and heard the events that he wrote down as the message from the Lord.

Day 2 • Obadiah

6. (a) The nations. (b) The Lord is sending them to battle against Edom.

7. The pride of Edom's heart deceived them; Edom had no understanding.

8. A soaring eagle brought down symbolizes the defeat of the nation. Thieves and grape harvesters represent the plundering armies that would make off with Edom's goods.

9. The "wise men" are responsible for the leadership they provide, and they would also face God's judgment for leading the people astray.

10. Still today, the Lord holds leaders responsible for their teaching and example. His wrath is still against those who lead others astray. The apostle Paul writes that the Lord Jesus triumphed over and disarmed "the rulers and authorities," which were probably demonic powers that would deceive the nations. Jesus triumphed by the calamity of His cross and the victorious resurrection, through which we receive the forgiveness of our sins.

Day 3 • Obadiah 10–14 and Malachi 1:2–5

11. Edom would be cut off forever; the Lord would be angry with the Edomites forever. God's judgment can be unrelenting against those who refuse His Word and blessing.

12. Answers will vary. Possible examples of commands and their revisions: Do not gloat over your brother's misfortune; do not say "I told you so" when someone else fails. Do not rejoice in the day of their ruin; do not laugh when someone goes bankrupt. Do not boast in the day of distress; do not toot your own horn. Do not enter the gate of My people; do not take advantage of others when they are down. Do not loot his wealth; do not steal from others. Do not stand at the crossroads to cut off the fugitives; do not trip someone who is trying

to escape his or her mistakes. Do not hand over the survivors; do not betray people.

13. Answers will vary. Do encourage those who fail. Do defend someone who suffers loss. Do hold your tongue until you have something positive to say. Do lift up those who have fallen into trouble. Do protect the income of others. Do support those going through a hard time. Do remain loyal to those who need a friend.

14. The Lord Jesus, who would become the Savior of all nations, would be born from the royal line of Judah. Ironically, it was Herod, an Idumean (Edomite), who sought to execute the baby Jesus, though the Lord preserved His life for our sakes.

Day 4 • Obadiah 15–18

15. The earlier verses were focused on one nation: Edom. Now the Lord and His prophet bring all nations into view. These verses also direct the Judeans' attention to the future.

16. You reap what you sow. You get the same treatment you have shown to others.

17. The inhabitants of Zion would escape the present troubles, and Zion would again be holy. They would inherit again their possessions. What is more, they would conquer Edom.

18. They will become fire and flame to burn up the house of Esau/Edom.

19. The people would be drawn to the Lord and become followers of Him, losing their national identity and former gods.

Day 5 • Obadiah 19–21

20. The tribal names indicate that a tribe or tribes is meant by those others who are mentioned. The tribe that certainly lived in the region of the Negeb and the Shephelah was Judah, though others might also settle among them, such as the Levites and Manassehites mentioned in 1 Chronicles.

21. Although the judges in Israel might serve for life, they also sometimes served as temporary military deliverers or "saviors."

22. The kingdom as a whole would belong to the Lord, who surpasses all other saviors.

23. **Challenge question.** The Lord currently reigns over the Church and the universe, but the fullness of His dominion is yet to come, when He will subdue all things that hinder His gracious reign: sin, death, and the devil. That is why He teaches us yet to pray, "Your kingdom come."

Arise, Go to Nineveh
Jonah 1

Preparing for the Session

Central Focus

God is everywhere. It is foolish to try to flee from Him. Rather than running from the Lord, we can find comfort in knowing that He is always there for His people.

Objectives

That participants, led by the Holy Spirit working through God's Word, will

1. accept their roles as workers in God's kingdom;
2. follow God's guidance in their lives; and
3. recognize the need for regular study of the Scriptures.

For the Small-Group Leader

Small-Group Discussion Helps

Day 1 • 2 Kings 14:23–29

1. Jonah was from the Northern Kingdom of Israel. He lived at Gath-hepher, in the region of the tribe of Naphtali. The king of Israel was Jeroboam II. Jeroboam II did what was evil in the eyes of the Lord, including the idolatrous worship introduced by Jeroboam I back in the time after the death of Solomon. The Lord showed Jonah that the borders of Israel from Lebo-hamath as far as the Sea of the Arabah would be restored to Israel.

2. Even though the people were in rebellion against the Lord, He sent His prophet to them and had mercy on them through King Jeroboam II.

3. *For personal reflection. Sharing optional.* Answers may vary. Jonah ministered at a time when he certainly faced opposition from false prophets and evil rulers. Yet he delivered the Lord's Word, leaving us an encouraging example to speak up.

Day 2 • Jonah 1

4. Doves and pigeons were among the clean animals offered in sacrifice to the Lord, which was pleasing to Him. We shall see in 1:12 that Jonah offers his life so that the Lord will calm the sea and save the sailors (1:12). From the belly of the great fish, Jonah offers his "voice of thanksgiving" in sacrifice to the Lord (2:9). In the New Testament the Lord calls us to present our selves as "a living sacrifice" (Romans 12:1).

5. Jonah was not faithful to the Lord's calling but ran away.

6. Jonah is in rebellion against the Lord, like Adam and Eve in the Garden of Eden after they had eaten the forbidden fruit and like Cain after he murdered his brother Abel. He might likewise have been afraid.

7. Answers may vary. Obvious answers include prayer (which is a response to Gods speaking to us; Psalm 145:18), reading the Bible, hearing God's Word at church, and especially attending the Sacrament of Christ's body and blood.

8. *For personal refection. Sharing optional.* Answers will vary. As time allows, invite participants to talk about the help they most need from the Lord. At all times, but especially when we don't know what to pray about, we may use the Lord's Prayer.

Day 3 • Jonah 1:4–6

9. **Challenge question.** Nothing happens without God allowing it. However, that does not mean that every so-called natural disaster is "an act of God" as some insurers state. In the case of Job, Satan was the one who sought an opportunity to test Job by causing him to suffer, though the Lord allowed that suffering to take place.

10. Because all people are sinners by nature, God is not obligated to restrain His wrath in their presence. Yet it is the case here that the sailors suffered unique hardship because of their interaction with Jonah, the Lord's servant.

11. Without genuine faith, their prayers could not please God. It is quite evident that at least some sailors were seeking the blessing of other gods, which made them idolaters.

Day 4 • Jonah 1:7–10

12. Lots were small gaming objects that when cast down would provide answers to the questions of the person

who cast them. We don't know exactly what these lots were like in Israel, though items like dice have been found in other nations.

13. Although Jonah acknowledges that he is a Hebrew, Jonah does not explain which land he comes from or what he does for a living, though he does make know that he was fleeing from the Lord (v. 10).

14. "Fear" in this case refers to something positive rather than to terror. To fear the Lord is to trust in Him for fulfillment of His promises and for forgiveness.

15. Jonah confesses that the Lord is God of heaven, God of the sea, and God of the dry land—one God for all locations.

16. Jonah just said that the Lord is God who made the sea and dry land. Jonah can't flee from the mighty Creator!

Day 5 • Jonah 1:11–16

17. Answers may vary. Jonah tells the sailors to throw him into the stormy sea, which would normally result in certain death. Jonah does express confidence that the Lord will supply a miraculous calm (v. 12), so He continues to confess the Lord's mighty power to save (in this case, deliverance from the storm for the sailors).

18. The sailors do not want to perish for someone else's sins, but they also fear that God will blame them for Jonah's death.

19. *For personal reflection. Sharing optional.* Answers will vary. Participants might respond like the sailors and pray fervently. However, at times, God's people do not turn to the Lord in prayer when faced with surpassing needs. Although this might convey confidence on behalf of some people, it likely indicates an indifference to God's promise to hear and answer our prayers.

20. Verse 16 tells us that the sailors feared to the point of making offerings and vows. Verse 16 does not tell us whether these sailors abandoned their other gods.

Jonah's Prayer and Preaching

Jonah 2–3

Preparing for the Session

Central Focus

At any time of the day or night, even in seemingly impossible circumstances, the Lord, who neither slumbers nor sleeps, is ready and willing to hear our prayers and deliver us in our needs.

Objectives

That participants, led by the Holy Spirit working through God's Word, will

1. be strengthened in their prayer life;

2. believe the Bible's accounts of the miracles of Jonah in the fish and Christ resurrected from the grave; and

3. appreciate the power of the Word to change people's hearts.

For the Small-Group Leader

Small-Group Discussion Helps

Day 1 • Jonah 1:17–2:9

1. God planned for Jonah's rescue, though in an unexpected way.

2. Answers may vary. The English translations that have "fish" faithfully reflect what the Hebrew says. Yet one may also note that the Hebrew word would not necessary exclude a whale. The word is not a strictly defined scientific term but a word for the finned creatures living in the water, which typically also had scales. Accuracy is, of course, important, but one needs to understand the culture that delivers the story to us.

3. *For personal reflection. Sharing optional.* Answers may vary. We tend to pray at set times and places rather than according to our needs. Jonah prays in the weirdest circumstances of all, which challenges us to stop holding back and start praying at all times. Jonah confesses that the Lord heard and answered him, even though the Lord did not immediately deliver him. That should inspire us to keep calling out to the Lord even when the answer does not appear right away.

4. Jonah refers to the belly of "Sheol," which is the place of the dead in the Old Testament, sometimes rendered as "the grave" or even as a place of punishment, such as "hell."

5. Jonah learned and confessed that the Lord hears and answers—and that He can even answer those who are in the belly of Sheol. God isn't just in heaven, His presence extends to all creation.

Day 2 • Jonah 2:3–4 and 2 Chronicles 7:11–16

6. (a) Jonah 1:15 mentions that the sailors cast Jonah into the sea; but in 2:3, it is the Lord who casts him in, showing that Jonah believed God was at work in all these events. (b) The waves and billows belong to the Lord. (c) Even at the worst time of Jonah's experience, the Lord is at work to accomplish His purposes for His prophet.

7. Jonah, while buried in the sea, states that he would again visit the holy temple in Jerusalem.

8. This passage records God's promise to hear His people whenever they would pray toward His temple. It is a prayer of repentance to "turn from their wicked ways."

Day 3 • Jonah 2:5–10

9. "The land" and "the pit" are references to Sheol, which was mentioned earlier in 2:2 (question 4).

10. Answers may vary. Jonah describes himself entering the realm of the dead, "whose bars closed" upon him forever. His life was definitely "fainting away," but he was also rescued.

11. The story of Jonah was a sign that Jesus would be in the grave for three days but would rise from the dead.

12. One abides in God's steadfast love by forsaking vain idols and trusting in the Lord alone.

13. Jonah turned to the temple when he set his heart to pray. Our times of prayer at church are training for those moments in life when death surrounds us. They teach us to speak our thanks to God as a sacrifice of praise for His salvation. Our confidence in Him likewise leads us to vow our service to Him.

Day 4 • Jonah 3

14. Nineveh was a huge city, three days' journey in breadth and with a population of about 120,000 persons, as well as their cattle. It was ruled by a king and by nobles who directed the population through their decrees. These rulers also led by example. Nineveh had evil ways in the Lord's eyes.

15. Jonah's message was that in forty days, Nineveh would be overthrown.

16. The people of Nineveh repented by holding a fast and putting on sackcloth. Everyone did this, not just some of the people.

17. *For personal reflection. Sharing optional.* Answers may vary. Be sure to emphasize that the Lord works through us and through our words to accomplish His good purposes.

18. *For personal reflection. Sharing optional.* Answers will vary. Answers will vary but should include words calling someone to repentance or encouraging them to trust in the Lord's mercy.

Day 5 • Jonah 3:6–10

19. The king removed his robe, put on sackcloth, and sat in ashes. He issued a proclamation, along with the nobles, that called on the entire community to join them in repentance and in prayer.

20. (a) Animals in sackcloth would naturally be irritable, bleating and mooing continually. (b) The cries of the animals would serve as a constant reminder of the people's need to repent and to abide in those activities. All normal activities would cease.

21. The king hoped that the Lord would relent and turn away from His fierce anger that would cause the people to perish.

22. The Lord turned from His plans to destroy Nineveh. The same expression is sometimes translated as "repented" to express the dramatic turn in God's mind from wrath to mercy. However, we typically associate repentance with sin, which is not part of God's character, so the word "relented" better serves our understanding of what God is doing.

Should Not I Pity Nineveh?
Jonah 4

Preparing for the Session

Central Focus

Self-centeredness and prejudices against others are deeply ingrained in sinful human nature, even among those who serve the Lord, and yet God would have us know that His boundless love extends to all people.

Objectives

That participants, led by the Holy Spirit working through God's Word, will

1. see in Jonah's anger their own prejudices;
2. marvel at God's grace toward this fallen world; and
3. reach out to all with God's love in Christ.

For the Small-Group Leader

Small-Group Discussion Helps

Day 1 • Jonah 4

1. Jonah knew the Lord would have mercy on the Assyrians, and he did not want them to receive God's mercy.

2. Jonah said, "O Lord, is not this what I said when I was yet in my country?" In other words, Jonah had already complained to God that he did not want the Assyrians to receive mercy, a fact not related at the beginning of the book.

3. The people first demanded and then worshiped a golden calf. In response, Moses cast down and broke the tablets of the Commandments before the people. After the people were punished and repented, the Lord showed Himself to Moses and made a covenant with the people.

4. Answers might fit in or be repeated in several categories. God sought to have mercy on the Ninevites. He likewise delivered Jonah from death. God might have given up on Jonah and chosen someone else, but instead He persisted with His wayward prophet. God demonstrated love for Jonah, for the people of Nineveh, and even for the cattle of Nineveh. He did not destroy the city. He rescued Jonah from Sheol.

Day 2 • Jonah 4:3–4

5. Moses offered himself unto damnation if the Lord would deliver Israel on his behalf. In contrast, Jonah would rather die than witness God's mercy for Nineveh. Moses acted with self-sacrificing care; Jonah acted from selfish motives.

6. Jonah's prayer should be "O Lord, have mercy on Nineveh. Do not hold their sins against them but rather hold them against me."

7. *For personal reflection. Sharing optional.* Answers will vary. Allow participants to share their thoughts and stories as time allows.

Day 3 • Jonah 4:5–6

8. Jonah wanted to stick around to see whether God would really spare the city or whether it might finally be destroyed.

9. God provided the plant to shade Jonah's head, "to save him from his discomfort."

10. **Challenge question.** The basic meaning of the word is "evil." The word described Jonah's standing before the Lord in that Jonah was not just uncomfortable due to the heat; his heart was evil before God because he could not stand to see God's compassion given for the Ninevites.

Day 4 • Jonah 4:7–8

11. God appointed a worm to attack the plant and He appointed the hot east wind and the sun to beat down on Jonah.

12. Today, Jonah might be described as depressed.

13. The Lord appointed the plant as an object lesson, to teach Jonah that his attitude was evil. Now the Lord shows Jonah that he has more concern for a plant than for a city full of people and cattle.

14. God may work through the events in our lives in unanticipated ways. Although we should be careful about finding divine meaning and intent in everything we experience, we should also pray that the Lord would help us understand the events of our lives in view of His Word, especially in view of His gracious and good will.

15. Everything we have is from the Lord, who may use our gifts and possessions for His purposes. Even if the Lord takes everything away, we may pray with Job, "Blessed be the name of the LORD."

Day 5 • Jonah 4:9–11

16. Jonah did not labor for the plant or make it grow, and the plant went away just as fast as it sprang up.

17. (a) God, by His own admission, should have compassion on Nineveh. (b) From the start of the book, God set out to have compassion. Jonah even confesses that is the nature of God (4:2).

18. God evidently wants to have compassion even on notorious sinners and wayward prophets. Yet clearly He allows people to resist His will, as was the case with Jonah. People who fail to receive God's salvation have hardened themselves against God's Word. Yet why some come to faith and others do not remains a mystery that even the story of Jonah cannot finally solve for us.

19. Answers will vary. People may be inspired by the fact that God drives the mission. He wants to save Nineveh, and He wants to work through a weak and even rebellious person to do so. If God can work through Jonah, He may also work through me.

The Lord Is Coming
Micah 1

Preparing for the Session

Central Focus

There is nothing new under the sun. People today, as in ancient times, still need the message of God's Law to show them their sin and the Gospel to show them their salvation.

Objectives

That participants, led by the Holy Spirit working through God's Word, will

1. pay attention to Scripture's warnings;

2. compare the idolatry of Micah's time with that of today; and

3. distinguish ever more clearly between Law and Gospel.

For the Small-Group Leader

Small-Group Discussion Helps

Day 1 • Micah 1; 2 Chronicles 27:1–28:4; 28:22–29:2

1. Jotham did what was right in the eyes of the Lord. However, the people still followed corrupt practices. He fought with the Ammonites, defeated them, and collected tribute. Ahaz did not do what was right in the eyes of the Lord. He imitated the ways of the kings of Israel who worshiped idols such as Baal. Shockingly, he even offered his sons as sacrifices. Later, after the Syrians defeated him, he began to worship the Assyrian gods, thinking they would help him. He cut up the vessels of the Jerusalem temple and even closed up the temple, suspending all services! Hezekiah did what was right in the eyes of the Lord. He reopened the temple.

2. Micah endured through the worst times in Judah, when Ahaz fully rejected the ways of the Lord and prevented his subjects from seeking the Lord at the temple. Micah must have been a brave and steadfast person to have endured under such circumstances.

3. While Isaiah was based in Jerusalem, the capital of Judah, Micah was from the outlying town of Moresheth. Isaiah's call began in the days of Uzziah, before Micah began to minister. Micah stated that he saw the "word of the Lord" regarding Samaria as well as Jerusalem. Isaiah saw visions especially about Judah and Jerusalem.

Day 2 • Micah 1:2–5a

4. Micah would prophesy regarding the whole earth.

5. God Himself would visit the earth.

6. God is responding to the transgressions and sins of Israel and Judah.

7. God will use the temple like a court of law to judge His people and the entire earth.

8. Assyria captured Samaria and carried the Israelites away into exile. Babylon captured Jerusalem, the king and his court, and took the people of Judah away to Babylon.

Day 3 • Micah 1:5b–7

9. Samaria was founded by Omri, an evil king of Israel who excelled in evil beyond his predecessors.

10. (a) High places were places where offerings were made to idols, which provoked God to anger. (b) God is coming down upon the high places to render judgment because the people were sacrificing to false gods on the high places.

11. The Lord would turn the shiny new capital into a heap of ruins, a hill for planting vines, and only the foundations would be left in place.

12. Samaria had grown prosperous on the fees for prostitution, which likely refers to the sacred prostitutes that served at pagan temples.

Day 4 • Micah 1:8–9

13. (a) The speaker is most likely the prophet Micah. (b) The Lord would not go about stripped and naked.

14. The prophet Micah is stripped in order to express his mourning for the people of Jerusalem. Isaiah laid aside

his clothes as a sign that the Assyrians would capture and humiliate the Egyptians and Cushites.

15. The idolatrous sins of Israel have also come to Judah and have corrupted the people, making them subject to God's wrath.

Day 5 • Micah 1:10–16

16. (a) David did not want the death of Saul, the first king of Israel, and of his sons, the princes of Israel, to be known in Gath, a city of the Philistine enemies. (b) Through Micah, God warns that just as the Philistines had conquered Saul's army in 2 Samuel, a new conqueror would come upon Israel and Judah.

17. These plays on words bitterly mock the stunning suffering the people would experience.

18. Answers will vary. Since the Lord inspired the very words Micah wrote and used his dark humor, the Lord could certainly allow preachers today to use dark humor as well. Yet preachers must be careful about turning the pulpit into a point of mockery by subjecting their hearers to excessive rhetoric. As in most things, some balance is required.

19. (a) There is no one like our Lord! As we saw earlier in the Book of Jonah, He is gracious and merciful, slow to anger, and abounding in steadfast love. (b) Answers will vary. Even disasters in our lives could not separate us from the grace of God (Romans 8:31–39).

Gather the Remnant

Micah 2–3

Preparing for the Session

Central Focus

Where is one to put his or her trust? To place one's trust in other human beings is foolish; God alone delivers when it comes to life on earth and in the world to come.

Objectives

That participants, led by the Holy Spirit working through God's Word, will

1. look to the almighty God, not earthly leaders, for assurance;

2. avoid false teachers who lead people astray; and

3. humble themselves before the Lord.

For the Small-Group Leader

Small-Group Discussion Helps

Day 1 • Micah 2:1–5

1. Micah addresses the people's coveting of other people's property and inheritance.

2. (a) The Lord gave Israel the lands on either side of the Jordan through the conquests led by Moses and Joshua. Moses had first given the lands beyond (east of) the Jordan to Reuben, Gad, and the half-tribe of Manasseh. Joshua divided the land west of the Jordan for the remaining tribes by casting lots. (b) The land was God's gift to them because of His covenant with the patriarchs. One might also note that the principle of inheritance also emphasized the role of the family in Israel.

3. The Lord is not evil, and He does no evil, for He cannot sin. But He does send hardship into our lives and uses it for bringing us to repentance and for bringing about His good purposes.

4. The Israelites are called by God to love, care, and provide for one another in this most basic societal relationship of husband with wife, parents with children.

Day 2 • Micah 2:6–13

5. (a) The Israelites do not want the prophet to preach about disgrace. (b) They wanted to hear sermons about wine and strong drink, most likely referring to the abundance of harvests that allowed for such beverages.

6. The Lord longs to do good to His people. That is His true and sincere nature. He wants them to be His dear, upright people.

7. There will be only a remnant left—not everyone would survive. The text likely refers to the coming exiles in Assyria and Babylon. However, the people will be together. God will open the breach that brings them out. He will be their king who leads them.

8. They remind us that not everyone abides in the faith. Some fall away. They also describe how the Lord would draw us together and lead us. Although one can be a Christian without a congregation, just as a sheep can be a sheep without the flock, it is not good (cf. Hebrews 10:24–25. We long for fellowship with our Lord and with one another.

9. Answers may vary. One might note that, rather than letting us stay on an over-grazed and dung-filled field, the Lord prepares for us a proper pasture where we belong and share in His abundant love.

Day 3 • Micah 3:1–4

10. (a) The fundamental problem is that the people hate the good and love the evil. (b) They have made their deeds evil. This is Micah's way of describing the effects of original sin in the people's lives.

11. The people are fighting with one another and taking advantage of one another, devouring up one another's goods and lives.

12. Micah is thinking of the coming exiles under the Assyrians and Babylonians.

13. We know God's justice from His good Word. In Israel's case, this would be through the covenant established through Moses. Justice in this passage has to do with fairness, that the people would not take advantage of one another and devour one another.

Day 4 • Micah 3:5–8

14. (a) These prophets are motivated by rewards of food. They are belly prophets who don't truly have and follow God's Word. (b) Those who serve merely for personal gain are treading the path of these prophets. This, of course, does not mean that fair pay should be withheld from church workers (remember vv. 1–3!).

15. (a) The false prophets will be disgraced because they will have no answer from God. (b) Answers may vary. Once we lose the Word of God, we lose the source of all spiritual blessings. Spiritual starvation naturally follows.

16. (a) Micah is filled with power, with the Spirit, with justice, and with might. He has the very Word of God to declare to the people. (b) *For personal refection. Sharing optional.* Answers will vary. Participants may wish to write or speak a prayer for the resource(s) they desire. They might also pray for one another.

Day 5 • Micah 3:9–12

17. Micah addresses the leadership of the people, gathered at the capital and even at the temple, which would be the pinnacle of the spiritual life in Judah. The fact that corruption reigns here among them reveals how desperate things have become.

18. (a) The leaders want a bribe, a price, and money. (b) Answers may vary. The universal and timeless interest in financial gain, which yields protection against others and power over them, is always at play among us. "You cannot serve God and money" (Matthew 6:24).

19. In this passage, the prophet rebukes the people for depending on the Lord falsely, stating that they have nothing to worry about because the Lord is present. This is God as a token or charm rather than as a Savior. When we depend on God for His Word, which leads us to repentance, true faith, and a new life, we are rightly leaning on the Lord.

20. The leaders in Jerusalem are expressing misplaced faith during a time of prosperity. Their faith does not affect their deeds. In contrast, Paul expresses faith in the Lord's deliverance at a moment of dire threat (some participants might recall that Paul wrote 2 Timothy while in prison; it is his last letter before execution). Paul has not just his earthly life in view but also his eternal destination in heaven.

Walk in the Name of the Lord

Micah 4–5

Preparing for the Session

Central Focus

God is faithful. Through the holy prophets, He made promises in the Old Testament that found their fulfillment in Jesus Christ in the New Testament; His Word is always sure, and it never fails.

Objectives

That participants, led by the Holy Spirit working through God's Word, will

1. patiently await the accomplishment of God's plans;
2. compare Old Testament prophecies with New Testament fulfillment; and
3. walk more closely with the Lord.

For the Small-Group Leader

Small-Group Discussion Helps

Day 1 • Micah 4

1. (a) Zion is described as the highest of the mountains. People from many nations will flow to it for learning. (b) Verse 2 introduces the cause with the word "for." The Law and the Word of the Lord will transform Zion and draw in the nations.

2. **Challenge question.** Answers may vary. The Soviets and United Nations used these words as an appeal for peaceful relations during the Cold War. However, the prophet Micah was thinking of the role of God's Word in judging the nations, which would bring about not just an end to cold war but the everlasting peace that only God could bring about.

3. Walking in the name of the Lord means living according to God's ways blamelessly and justly, keeping His covenant.

4. Although God's Word went forth at the time of Jesus, and prospers among the nations now, the peace and joy that Micah describes can reach fulfillment only in eternity after Jesus returns.

Day 2 • Micah 4:6–8

5. Micah refers to the remnant and says that the time of healing will be "from this time forth" so that it is not limited to the New Testament era but could begin right away. God always wants to bless His people.

6. Yes. Micah says so explicitly. God both allows hardships to come into our lives and at times causes hardship to come into our lives. But not every hardship we experience comes from God. The devil, the world, and our own sinful nature may also bring hardships.

7. "Remnant" is parallel with "a strong nation" in Micah's poetry, so Micah envisions the remnant as blessed and restored.

8. (a) Zion is a tower for watching over and protecting the flock. (b) The Church is the new Zion, established by the Lord for blessing His people.

Day 3 • Micah 4:9–13

9. Judah had a king at the time that Micah was writing, but many of Judah's kings did what was evil in the sight of the Lord. The Lord was the real king and ruler for God's people, despite Judah's earthly leadership. So Judah always had her heavenly King, though they too often ignored Him.

10. The imagery in verse 11 refers to rape—violent, terrifying, and defiling. The captured Judeans likely suffered such outrage as well as the loss of their property and their dignity in slavery.

11. God has a plan for Zion and its people. The nations cannot discern how God is at work in the midst of all this suffering.

12. The Lord has gathered the nations not to destroy Zion but to despoil the nations. The wealth of the nations would become offerings to the Lord, as has happened through the Church that reaches all nations.

13. Answers may vary. We can take comfort knowing that the Lord is everywhere present and provides in every way for His dear people, even though we face struggles and suffering in this world (Romans 8:28). In Judah's case, this would mean its renewal as a nation after the exile and its role in providing the Messiah for the salvation of all people.

Day 4 • Micah 5:1–6

14. The "daughter of Zion," Jerusalem and its outlying towns, must gather its troops for self-defense. The "judge of Israel" is a title for the king of Judah.

15. (a) This prophecy describes the birth of Jesus, who would become ruler of Israel and even of the nations. He was born "king of the Jews." (b) Jesus is eternal, true God.

16. "She" is Mary, and "His brothers" are the people of Israel who would become disciples of Jesus.

17. Rather than Judah delivering itself through its great leaders, the Lord delivered Judah through the prayers of Hezekiah. The Lord sent His angel to cut off the Assyrians.

Day 5 • Micah 5:7–15

18. (a) The remnant would be like "dew" and "showers," refreshing and encouraging others. (b) The remnant would also be like a lion, powerful against its adversaries.

19. The feast of Purim celebrated the Judeans' defeat of their enemies throughout the provinces where they were scattered.

20. (a) The Lord would provide His Word and Law. He would judge the nations so that they experience peace and prosperity. He would also execute vengeance on the disobedient nations. (b) He would take away their weapons. From their enemies, He would take away war horses, chariots, cities, strongholds, sorceries, idols.

21. *For personal reflection. Sharing optional.* Answers will vary. Provisions should include the blessings of Word, Sacraments, prayer, and congregational fellowship. Things taken away should include the removal of sins, discouragement, doubt, and the like.

Walk Humbly with Your God

Micah 6

Preparing for the Session

Central Focus

Throughout history, the Lord has showered His people with blessings, and He will continue to be with us forever. Yet the history of those who have rejected Him serves as a warning against unbelief.

Objectives

That participants, led by the Holy Spirit working through God's Word, will

1. remember God's workings in the past;
2. understand that God's judgments are always just; and
3. practice justice and kindness toward others.

For the Small-Group Leader

Small-Group Discussion Helps

Day 1 • Micah 6

1. "The Lord our God, the Lord is one. You shall love the Lord your God will all your heart and with all your soul and with all your might." It also explains to Israel how they are to remember and teach the Word of the Lord.

2. (a) Micah appeals to His people, Israel. (b) He is indicting Israel for forgetting what the Lord had done for them. They had become weary with the Lord and stopped listening to Him.

3. The mountains and hills. In other words, the land that the Lord gave them is now to judge them.

4. The land would vomit out the Canaanites because of their unclean acts. If Israel adopted the same or similar practices, they, too, would be vomited out.

Day 2 • Micah 6:3–5

5. The Lord did good to them, giving them His covenant, deliverance, and the Promised Land

6. Israel was bored with following the covenant and wanted to adopt the practices of the nations.

7. The passage echoes the opening words of the Ten Commandments, where the Lord states, "I am the Lord your God, who brought you out of the land of Egypt, out of the house of slavery" (Exodus 20:2).

8. Balak intended to have Balaam curse Israel, which would have led to their destruction.

9. Balaam, who intended to curse Israel, instead blessed them because he could not do otherwise than what the Lord commanded him. His blessings reveal that the Lord will make Israel a great nation that would crush Moab, Edom, and others.

Day 3 • Micah 6:6–8

10. Micah is asking how he can please God.

11. Micah refers to entering the temple courts before the altar of burnt offerings where every man in Israel was to bring the annual sacrifices.

12. God is greater, higher, and beyond us. Although the temple was the ideal place to come "before the Lord" in the Old Testament, the Lord is present everywhere and we may call upon Him and come before Him at all times and places. In the New Testament, we are specially drawn to Jesus as the temple of the Lord (cf. John 2:19).

13. What the Lord really wants is for His people to "do justice, and to love kindness, and to walk humbly with your God."

14. *For personal reflection. Sharing optional.* Answers will vary but should include examples of justice/fairness, kindnesses, and ways in which a person will serve humbly.

Day 4 • Micah 6:9–15

15. Micah speaks against the use of scant measures, wicked scales, deceitful weights, violence, lies, deceit, sins, the statutes of Omri, the works of the house of Ahab, and walking in the counsels of Ahab's house.

16. These are sins especially of the marketplace and of city-based administrations.

17. The people would lose the fruit of their labors.

18. The prophet mentions "sound wisdom to fear [His] name" (6:9).

19. Answers will vary. The prayer should celebrate God's gift of wisdom, manifest especially in sending Jesus Christ as the living Word who blesses us with the light of the knowledge of God.

Day 5 • Micah 6:16

20. Omri did evil in God's sight, followed the way of Jeroboam in worshiping idols, and provoked the Lord with his sin.

21. Ahab married Jezebel the Sidonian, worshiped Baal, built an altar and temple for Baal at Samaria, made an Asherah, and did more to provoke the Lord than anyone before him.

22. Jehoshaphat made a marriage alliance with Ahab, so that one or more of his children married persons in Ahab's family. Since the two families were thus related, they joined forces for war against other nations. Jehoshaphat helped "the wicked and love[d] those who hate[d] the LORD" (2 Chronicles 19:2).

23. The Lord intended to make Judah a desolation, hissing, and scorn.

24. In Esther 9, the sounds include feasting, gladness, and holiday activities.